DUST & DRAMA

DUST & DRAMA

75 years of live theatre in Broken Hill

MARILYN HARRIS

To order additional copies of this book, contact:
Xlibris
1-800-455-039
www.Xlibris.com.au
Orders@Xlibris.com.au
790026

CONTENTS

Preface

Having listened to many stories from Doug Jones and others, I was inspired to collect stories from present and former associates of Broken Hill Repertory Society for inclusion in a book we could all enjoy.

Doug Jones had researched the Broken Hill City Library archives and compiled a short history of the society, which he read to those who attended the fiftieth anniversary celebration of Theatre 44 opening, in July 2013.

My contribution to the celebrations was the scanning and compiling of all the photos included in the archives. These were included in PowerPoint presentations that were shown on the day. They have now been assembled in a series of collages that hang in the Theatre 44 foyer, and the collages have been printed in this book.

Unfortunately, between the years 1984 and 2004 there were some turbulent times, and complete records were not kept. Before 1984 each play included a photo shoot of each actor and these were retained in the archives. After 1984 few photos were taken and archived. Quite a bit of effort has gone into listing many of the productions in this period, but it would need more time and the input of more people, many of whom have left town, to complete the records. If you can contribute anything further to our records, please contact me.

So many people have been involved in and formed an attachment for the Repertory Society and Theatre 44 over the seventy-five years of its existence. The experience of rehearsing and performing has drawn people together (indeed a number of permanent relationships have sprung from this experience) and built their confidence.

Wherever people spend a lot of time together achieving, there are always interesting and funny stories and memories. So while this book covers the history of the Broken Hill Repertory Society, it includes many funny anecdotes and tributes that will be of interest to members past and present.

Reader, please be aware that these memories are not definitive. We all remember things differently. So if there is a memory that does not seem right to you, please treat us kindly.

Marilyn Harris
Editor

A Short History of Broken Hill Repertory Society Inc.

Prepared and read by Doug Jones at the fiftieth anniversary of Theatre 44 opening, 14 July 2013

Act 1: Ten Years Without Amateur Theatre

I went to the library a few months ago to get copies of the September 1963 *Barrier Miner* and *Barrier Daily Truth* articles on the opening of Theatre 44. I noticed a brief mention of Vic Bindley in the *Barrier Miner* article and, being vaguely aware that a Vic Bindley was a key figure in the formation of the Repertory Society (Rep), decided to trawl through the on-line records of the *National Library of Australia* and *Austage* to see what they had on him.

From these resources, I can give an overview of the events that led to the formation of Rep, which might sound like a Vic Bindley tribute. This is inevitable because he was a pivotal figure in those events. I will then look at why the board of directors decided in August 1962 to build the playhouse.

The amateur theatre scene in Broken Hill was bleak in the early 1940s, with some ten years passing since there had been a permanent amateur theatre organisation in Broken Hill. Lists of productions at the Crystal and Tivoli Theatres and the Town Hall reveal that all was not lost though, as revues and variety concerts were regularly staged and were popular.

Vic Bindley arrived in Broken Hill in 1942 to manage the cinema in Oxide Street which was then known as Johnson's Theatre.

He had previously managed the Civic and Mayfair Theatres in Sydney. But his value to live theatre in Broken Hill would be in his practical experience, which included set and lighting design for the J. C. Williamson theatre organisation, and in his enthusiasm for Repertory Theatre (a permanent theatre company, which would be amateur, and produce a succession of plays). Vic Bindley has been described as being 'creatively brilliant'.

The Broken Hill Repertory Society's origin could be said to have been in 1942 when a group of theatre-loving people banded together to raise funds for various war organizations. At the heart of this group of people were Vic Bindley, Pat Peoples and Bert Johns. A. J. Keast, the manager of the Zinc Corporation, was a keen supporter of the group.

Their first move was to form Silver City Players. That group immediately demonstrated that it would not take the easy option when it decided to stage 'Journey's End' by R. C. Sherriff for its first production in October 1942, with Vic Bindley directing.

'Journey's End' is set in the trenches during WW1, and is an intense war drama about something we do not think about - waiting. Vic Bindley was technician for the original Australian production of 'Journey's End', and devised additional effects for the local production to make it, as people who had seen either the original London or Australian productions said, superior to the original.

The dugout in which the play was performed was authentic in detail with a great deal of timbering and sandbagging, and the stage was covered with two to three inches of dirt to add to the realism. It needed ingenious construction as the dugout was shelled in the last scene and collapsed in a turmoil of timber, sandbags, and flying dirt.

'Journey's End' had full houses for its five performances at the Crystal Theatre. Given my vague recollection of the size of the Crystal Theatre, this was an impressive achievement.

After the success of 'Journey's End', Silver City Players was reformed as the Silver City Players' Club. This group was a step closer to Vic Bindley's vision of a repertory theatre, as it intended to stage a number of plays in a season.

Their first production was the popular musical 'The Desert Song' by Sigmund Romberg, directed by Vic Bindley, which opened on 14 August 1943 and ran for a week. Bindley must have called on his theatre contacts as this production featured the costumes from the original London production. The lavish scenic effects were designed and executed by Fred Jobson, who shares the creatively brilliant description with Vic Bindley. There was an orchestra - which was common in local productions – and a newspaper report mentioned it playing to a packed Crystal Theatre, with many people standing and two hundred turned away.

Not content with having just finished a successful season at the Crystal Theatre, the production team, cast and crew from 'The Desert Song' immediately began work on their revue, 'Sky High'. 'Sky High' was devised and produced by Vic Bindley, with Fred Jobson once again designing and executing lavish scenery. Sky High ran for four nights at the Crystal Theatre in November, 1943, with the generous performances finishing at 11.45 p.m.

Act II: Rep is formed

The short and enthusiastic lives of Silver City Players and Silver City Players' Club were the prologue to an important event. On 24 October 1944, a special meeting of people interested in the establishment of a repertory theatre movement was held at the Palace Hotel lounge in Argent Street.

The meeting was addressed by Vic Bindley, who said that he had been for some time investigating the possibility of establishing a repertory movement which would give full expression to local dramatic talent. The standard set by a small band of enthusiasts in the production of *'Journey's End'* convinced him such work could be carried out on a larger scale.

The foundation members of the Broken Hill Repertory Society met on 12 November, 1944, to elect the first board of directors. Vic Bindley, Pat Peoples, and Bert Johns presented the proposed constitution, rules and regulations. A. J. Keast was elected chairman. Bindley was appointed producer/director.

Bindley's vision was for a full-blooded repertory movement that would embrace every aspect of theatrical activity, including training in production and various aspects of stagecraft. He also stressed how the repertory movement kept alive the traditions of stage with flourishing interest and enthusiasm when the advent of sound on film seemed to indicate that the days of stage had gone forever.

The project was given a significant boost when the NSW Police Boys' Club authorities generously loaned their theatrette to the new theatre group free of cost.

The Rep production that possibly best allowed Vic Bindley to use his creative brilliance was *'The Fledglings'* (adapted and produced by Vic Bindley) in 1947.

The story of *'The Fledglings'* took place on one of the many small islands off the southern coast of New Guinea during the Second World War.

All the scenes took place in a native hut with a towering mountain, ack-ack battery, and airstrip visible through a large window upstage. Vic Bindley's creative genius had aircraft landing, taking off and flying around with realistic recorded sound effects, ack-ack firing and other visual and audio war effects. To top it all off there was a shower of rain downstage.

Stage-managing a Bindley production would have been a master class in technical theatre.

An interesting footnote is that, due to Bindley's commitments at the cinema, rehearsals of the early plays he directed for Rep would begin around 11p.m., and some of the cast would arrive with a thermos and mattress. And now people are reluctant to rehearse just a few times at a normal hour!

Vic Bindley retired from Rep at the AGM on 2 December 1948, due to the pressure of business and the demands of Rep overtaxing his health and strength.

He said that the production of six plays in 1948 had rested on eight members, and he was unable to give Rep the time required because of increased business responsibilities. This is understandable when it is considered that as producer/director Vic Bindley either directed or had oversight of the majority of the eighteen plays staged during his four active years with Rep. The good news was that by then, Rep was a vibrant little theatre group, well prepared to continue staging plays.

Act III: Decision to Build a Theatre

Rep complemented its productions in its early years with activities such as forming a play-reading group, taking a full production to Port Pirie, and recording two plays for ABC Radio, but I want to move on to the events that led to the construction of The Playhouse in 1963.

Before I do, I must acknowledge a Rep living treasure for being my muse in the preparation of this history and for her invaluable assistance when I was looking for information on the decision to build a theatre - Eleanor Williams.

While Rep had been given use of the Police Boys Club theatrette free of charge, the arrangements were for just the last few rehearsals and a few performances of each play to be held at the theatrette.

Rehearsals were initially held in the foyer of Johnson's Theatre after it closed for the night, then later moved to Pellew and Moore's theatre room in Argent Lane.

This became increasingly impractical as it was used as a workshop and paint shop as well as for rehearsals, and the Society obtained better rehearsal rooms in Wendt Chambers above what is now People's Chemist in Argent Street late in 1947.

The Wendt Chambers rehearsal room measured approximately seven metres by five metres, which was smaller than the theatrette stage, and became increasingly cramped as props were stored around the walls.

Eleanor recalls the rehearsal space being reduced to around six by four metres, and anyone with theatre experience will know that it would have been a huge challenge to rehearse in cramped conditions and then move the production onto the larger stage AND bed down the artistic and technical elements in just a few rehearsals.

Our intrepid thespians persevered despite these difficulties, and the Society started to attract many people from the community from the mid 1950s.

Many talented actors, directors, and backstage personnel emerged, and the number of performances per play gradually increased from two to five or six, as the standard of the productions attracted mounting interest.

It was becoming increasingly difficult for the Police Boys Club to accommodate Rep's need for more rehearsals on the stage and the extra performances. However, program notes as late as the fourth production in 1961 had an optimistic outlook as steady but sure progress was being made towards the rejuvenation of the theatrette.

The turning point was in August 1962, when the *Barrier Miner* reported that the board of directors had decided to build a theatre. Loans totalling fifteen thousand pounds were obtained from the ANZ Bank and the Mine Managers Association, and plans were prepared for the playhouse.

With their consent Eleanor Williams, Bob Cawdle, and Eric Minchin were appointed guarantors/trustees by the board of directors, with the responsibility to repay the loan if the members could not meet the commitment. Airlie Pedlar was appointed a guarantor/trustee following the death of Eric Minchin.

Construction of the playhouse commenced in March 1963, and it was opened by Mayor George Dial on 21 September 1963.

Vic Bindley, who was very much the catalyst for the revival of live theatre in Broken Hill and the formation of Rep, was looking forward to attending the opening of the playhouse. Sadly, he passed away on the weekend prior to the opening.

The Society later became an incorporated entity and, with the loans repaid, the trustees retired. We must acknowledge here the efforts of those dedicated Rep people - the various boards of directors, actors, and backstage workers - who worked so hard during the 1970s and 1980s to repay the loans in an increasingly competitive entertainment market.

Eleanor had a sparkle in her eyes recently when she told me that her proudest moment was standing on the stage of the new playhouse, looking out over the seats that came from a local cinema. Everyone who had a hand in making Rep the success it had become by 1963 should have been proud.

Our task is to honour those proud moments, and the great enthusiasm of all those people who made Rep and this place possible, by striving to ensure that the miracle of live theatre returns to these boards.

To do that, we might well have to start all over again by recapturing the skills and enthusiasm of those people who stared down the threat of sound on film and of that small group who started the whole theatre ball rolling in Broken Hill in 1942.

Eric Minchin

Bob Cawdle

Airlie Pedlar

The Show Must Go On - Break a Leg

Margot White

My earliest memories of the Repertory Society would be 1944, the year it all began. Plays were held at the Police Boys' Club in Railwaytown.

I was eleven years old, and my mother, Nydia Edes, was involved from the beginning of Repertory as she was very interested in theatre. She had a part in the second production, a play called 'The Women' by Clare Boothe Luce (1945).

I was a little too young to accompany Mum to rehearsals, However I remember the discussions at home of how late she would get home. I also remember her rehearsing her lines at home.

Victor Bindley was the driving force behind the early productions. He was producer and director and he guided and taught the crew everything from lighting, to sound, props, costume. He had so much experience of theatre.

The financial backing came from the mining companies, primarily Zinc Corporation and North Mine.

Victor Bindley was the manager of Johnson's Theatre (now Silver City Cinema). He had many years experience of live theatre working for J. C. Williamson's productions. His arrival in Broken Hill was met with enthusiasm and Broken Hill Repertory Society was born.

Mr Bindley's position as Picture Theatre manager meant he had to be in attendance at every showing. The evening movie ended at approximately 11.00p.m., and it was after that time that the Rep rehearsals would commence at the Police Boys Club. All of the cast and technicians were working, or were business people, so it was not possible to hold rehearsals in the day time.

Actors and crew were already rehearsing and awaiting Mr Bindley's arrival by car. Mr Bindley did not own a car, nor did he drive, so he had to rely on a crew member to pick him up and also drive him home.

Many a night a small-part player had to be roused from sleep to take the cue. In fact, on one occasion, a cast member found a quiet corner backstage after his last cue, and went to sleep. When it was lock up time it was assumed he had gone home. But no, he was locked in the Police Boys Club. The staff of PBC woke him from his sleep at about 8.00 a.m. next morning. He slept well.

My mother became very involved, and, although she had only one performance, she was appointed wardrobe mistress and remained in that role for many years.

Victor Bindley had a lady friend who was a professional dressmaker, and as she was a very busy lady, she did not have time to apply her sewing skills at Repertory. However, she made available her business premises for the use of sewing machines and cutting table and other sewing needs.

Apart from costumes, various other props had to be made such as curtains, cushions, etc. Rosa Birmingham also made her premises available to actors who needed to rehearse on occasions when PBC was not available, such as early evening and weekends.

Rosa's business was upstairs above what is now People's Chemist (previously Bon Marche) in Wendt's Chambers. I remember as I grew into my teens going to Rosa's on many occasions with Mum to help with the sewing. There is a photo with Mum at the cutting table and me at the machine, probably 1947-48.

Sometime in the mid 1950s I recall going to Rosa's to help with prompting when rehearsing for 'Dial M for Murder' by Frederick Knott (1956). I was never front of stage, but rather helped backstage.

The dressing rooms were downstairs, one for the females and one for the men with very cramped spaces. It was also a long way from the stage, and many a cue was nearly missed. Often a runner was needed to stand outside the building listening to the lines and calling for the cast member downstairs to hurry up. It was a very unpleasant job standing outside in the cold.

Many evenings over the years I was usherette and programme seller. I continued in this role until I was about twenty-five years old and after I had been married. There were many young girls willing to be usherettes and programme sellers and also plenty of staff to assist backstage, so I decided just to be a member and enjoy the shows.

My parents, along with my husband, continued to enjoy attending shows well after Rep moved to its new home in Wills Street and became renamed as Theatre 44. I guess I was a volunteer for about fifteen years.

Many producers and directors followed the Bindley era and the standard was maintained at a high level of theatre. Mr Bindley was a great man to work with and he passed on his knowledge freely. The backstage volunteers remained in their positions for many years. I remember Reg Armstrong, Alan Cornish, and Fred Jobson (for his superb artwork on the sets). There were others over the years whose names I cannot remember. They did the lighting, sound, curtain, set changes, props, and all the demands of Victor Bindley.

One of the finest actors was a young school teacher called Don Neville. His role in 'The Hasty Heart' by Captain John Patrick (1947) received a standing ovation and tears - it touched your heart.

Eugenie Bond in 'Madam Tic Tac' by Falkland L Carey was outstanding. Mary Anson, Cliff Neate, Pat Peoples, Margaret Morrison, Bert Johns, Mary Coddy, Max Middleton and Bob Cawdle, were a few early-day actors I remember.

Memorable producers were Margaret Hall, Eleanor Williams and Rosemary Brown, as well as pianist Val Gough. 'The King and I' was superb. So many to remember, and too many to include here. John Pickup and Mary Maguire were also great contributors.

'Amphitryon 38' by Jean Giraudoux (1948) was a challenging play, and the talented Fred Jobson created a wonderful set. The setting was in Roman times, and the set required marble columns and a parapet. Fred's artistic work on canvas created the marble columns that looked so real.

The night I attended the performance, an incident occurred that has remained in my memory. The scene was two actors standing on the parapet between two marble columns, looking down at the crowd below. The two actors were dressed in togas, and each carried a long staff. Cliff Neate was one of the actors, and I cannot remember who the other was. They were having a serious discussion. Cliff's line was, 'What dost thou see?' At that precise moment the power went out and the entire theatre was in darkness. Ooh's and aah's and silence. The other actor replied, 'Can't see a bloody thing!' There were roars of laughter from the audience and stage, and after several moments of hilarious banter from the stage, the power was restored. The scene then was Cliff laughing so much his toga was shaking in time with his tummy (he had a roundish figure), and his staff had become entangled with one 'marble' column. The sight of Cliff laughing and untangling himself from the marble nearly became a disaster. The laughter saved the night. The curtain closed - time to recover. The very serious play went on in true trooper style.

George Brooks, who was a board member and patron, was assistant manager at Zinc Corporation, and chairman of directors of the Repertory Society. He lived in a company residence in the Gypsum Street group, and his home was made available for after- last-performance parties. I was a little young to attend the early-day parties, but I attended a few when I was about seventeen years old. I don't recall much about them except sitting outside on a warm evening in the beautiful garden. The house was on an elevated site; a set of steps led down to the garden. I would sit on the top of the steps with a lemonade, looking at the floodlit garden. Not too many people my age attended. Mr and Mrs Brooks had a daughter, Barbara, who was not too many years older than me so I got to know her. Mum and Dad were there, and I remember that everyone enjoyed the parties. Goodness knows how or what time we went home. Sadly, the house has been demolished and the garden has gone.

From 1944 to 1949, Mum attended not all but many dress rehearsals, and I recall that it was difficult for her to get to the PBC at that awkward time. We did not own a car as it was war-time and post-war. Dad had to save his money and bought his first car in 1948. Mum decided she would learn to ride my school bike, so after a few wobbly lessons she managed to stay on. And off she went into the night. We lived in Wyman Street (north side), so it was a long way to Railwaytown. I do not think she ever rode a bike after 1948. If the weather was unsuitable for bike riding, she most likely arranged for a lift.

How the National Anthem Disappeared from Rep Productions

Doug Jones

When we went to the cinema in the early 1960s in Australia, we always stood for the national anthem (which was then '*God Save the Queen*') before the session began. I do not recall the national anthem being played before professional theatre productions, but it was played before all Broken Hill Repertory productions. This is the story of how the national anthem disappeared from Rep productions.

I was stage-managing for Rep in the late 1960s. About ten minutes before curtain time one night, the sound operator told me that the national anthem record was just about unplayable. I said 'In that case we would do without it'.

I was asked if I could make that decision and I pointed out that as stage manager I was in charge of performances on behalf of the board. This meant that when there was no time for a board meeting, I had to make a decision. We did not play the national anthem that night, and there was no comment from the board members who were present. The national anthem was never played again and the board was silent on the matter.

The practice of playing the national anthem at cinemas in Australia stopped around the early 1970s, so I suppose it could be said that Rep set the ball rolling!

The Case of the Micturating Camel

Doug Jones

One of the problems associated with staging pantomimes in Australia is that we do not have a panto tradition. While a script might say little more than 'Camel enters' and 'Camel exits', the people in the camel in British productions know how to do the silliness that makes panto fun.

We can check these things out now on You-Tube, but that resource was a long way in the future when Kate Finlayson recruited Doug Jones and Darryl Haynes to be the front and rear halves, respectively, of the camel for her 1972 production of 'Aladdin'. Darryl was an industrial arts teacher originally from Kansas, USA, and had the distinction of making his stage debut as the rear end of a camel.

The camel in that production had three scenes. The first involved the camel wandering on and sharing a couch with a rather surprised villain, Abanazar (played by Phil Cantwell). In its second appearance the camel went downstage and interacted with the audience, and its third appearance was in the final scene when the camel inflicted the final insult on the defeated evil Abanazar by sitting on him. The boys knew nothing about camels doing soft-shoe shuffles, leaning cross-legged against the proscenium and so on, so the camel was fairly bland at the final dress rehearsal.

Not much could be done to spice up the first entrance, but Doug and Darryl decided after the opening night that the interaction with the audience should extend to a lap of the auditorium. This included some lucky person sitting in an aisle seat having a camel sitting in their lap. The lucky person at one performance was George Connor, manager of the Zinc Mine. The look on George's face when he realised what the camel was up to was priceless, but he was a good sport.

Another lucky person was an occasional Rep actor who told the boys that the camel could not possibly get him because he was sitting in the middle of the second row from the cross aisle. Never tell a camel that something cannot be done!

The boys did not tell Kate about their plan to invade the audience, but the fact that they kept it short and the kids loved it meant that Kate was happy to let the camel visit the audience for the rest of the run.

The camel operators were also not satisfied with the camel walking on and nodding to the audience at the curtain call. They did some rather funny rehearsals backstage during the second performance, and surprised Kate by having the camel skip on and do a deep curtsey at the curtain call. The camel skipped on for the rest of the run. It is apparently not easy to skip in a camel costume!

The real fun for the camel happened on the last night, and was not a last-night prank: the boys merely seized on a random opportunity. As they were climbing into the camel costume for its final entrance Darryl pointed to a soda siphon on a props table in the wings. Doug nodded, and Darryl grabbed the siphon and took it under the rear of the costume. Several people in the wings asked what they were up to, but at that moment there wasn't a plan.

There was a plan when the camel went on stage. When the time came for the camel to sit on the wicked *Abanazar*, Doug and Darryl lined the camel up alongside *Abanazar* and then, after a pause for effect, the camel cocked its rear right leg and micturated on the unfortunate and very surprised *Abanazar* (OK, he peed on *Abanazar*!). And it was not the pathetic few drops of an elderly camel with prostate problems either; this was the fire hose job of a teenage camel.

The audience roared laughing which, apart from making the camel operators feel pretty good, also masked a rather naughty word said by Phil. The problem was that Phil was already on stage when the idea of using the soda-siphon arose, so there was no time to warn him that he would be peed on. On the other hand, perhaps Phil might not have been warned even if there had been time.

The cast loved the micturating camel and told Darryl and Doug after the curtain call that it was brilliant. The boys said that they were disappointed with it, prompting the cast to emphasise their love of what happened. The boys then said that they were disappointed that they did not think of it fifteen performances earlier.

Pantos seem to be the source of mischief. Peter Sweeney got a surprise in another panto in that era when his character opened the front of a grandfather clock during a performance, as he did in every performance, and discovered a *Cleo* centrefold sticky-taped inside. Let's just say that Peter did one of the most spectacular double takes seen on Rep stage.

A Naughty Word and a Pro Hart Painting

Doug Jones

The perfect storm occurred during a performance of Rep's 1968 production of *'Of Mice and Men'* by John Steinbeck. A lady in the audience was offended when one of characters said 'bastard', and entered the foyer at interval announcing to all present that she had a good mind to go home.

It so happened that there was an exhibition of Pro Hart paintings in the foyer, one of which was *'The Yabby Hunter'*. This painting showed a naked man in a billabong with a yabby rather painfully attached to a very sensitive part of the male anatomy. Madam stopped in front of this painting as she loudly considered going home, causing a couple of backstage workers, who were at the canteen getting drinks, to giggle because they could see what was going to happen.

Madam was once more declaring loudly that she had a good mind to go home when, mid sentence, she happened to glance at *'The Yabby Hunter'*..... "I AM going home", she declared, and off she went. It must be said that the language was perfectly in context given that *'Of Mice and Men'* is about ranch hands in rural USA.

Time Commitment - 'South Pacific' - 1965

Doug Jones

It is interesting to reflect on the amount of time people put into Rep during what could be called its golden era - which could be said to be the period prior to the arrival of television in Broken Hill. I have chosen 1965 as I was fortunate to be there and, therefore, have some inside knowledge and have also uncovered some information on that year.

There were seven performances of each of the five plays produced in 1965 and twenty performances of 'South Pacific', making a total of fifty five performances in that season. If we presume three rehearsals per week for ten weeks for each production, we have a minimum of thirty rehearsals for each production, or around 180 rehearsals for the whole season.

Front of House
I will start with the commitment of front of house people. House manager, Ron Herriman, would be at the door welcoming patrons to every performance and generally running a tight FOH ship. Other people would quietly and efficiently work on publicity and preparation of the programs for each production, operation of the foyer shop and the foyer board, and making the auditorium ready for each production.

Performers
Now we come to the performers. As we have seen above, performers in a play could expect a minimum of thirty rehearsals followed by

seven performances, while those in *South Pacific* would have had no less than thirty rehearsals followed by twenty performances.

A number of people were in more than one play, but the over achievers would have to have been Ross Lindeman and Frank McKone, who were involved in four productions. In Ross's case he acted in four productions, which means that he potentially attended up to 120 rehearsals and had twenty-eight performances.

Frank McKone was possibly a super over-achiever as he directed one of the four productions he was involved in.

The actual number of rehearsals attended by any actor depended on the rehearsal schedule for each act in a play.

Director
To put this into perspective, it is worth looking at Eleanor Williams' preparation when she was preparing a play. El told me that she would begin her preparation for a production some six months before the casting reading, in order that she could be prepared to guide the cast to the best production possible. Given a director with good theatre and people skills and a cast keen to be part of a good production, the long rehearsal process could be enjoyable. The point of this long rehearsal process was, of course, to make performing look easy.

All of this means that Frank put in a long year at Rep in 1965.

Backstage Crew
Now we come to those unsung and exceedingly modest hidden heroes of theatre – the backstage crew. The properties people and prompt were usually recruited by directors for their production, while the make-up, wardrobe, lighting, sound, set construction, decor and stage management teams worked on all six productions.

While casts, props, and prompts tended to vary from play to play, the set construction, lighting, sound, stage management, wardrobe and make-up teams went from production to production.

For the set construction crew, for instance, this meant building and pulling down six sets during the season. In my case, being part of the stage management team as well as the set construction crew, it meant that the commitment continued into the performances. But we loved it.

Sound Effects

Sound operator Ricky West was not satisfied with the available recorded aircraft sound effects when he was preparing the sound effects for Rep's 1966 production of 'South Pacific' by Rodgers and Hammerstein, so he did something that I doubt could be done these days.

Rick went to the local airport, where he had a chat with the air traffic controller on duty and the pilot of a DC-3 who happened to be there. The outcome of this chat was that Rick was able to set up his recording gear near the airstrip that the pilot intended to use and record the sound of the take-off. The helpful pilot turned after the take-off and flew low over Rick. With some clever editing and other sound operator tricks, Rick was able create very realistic and effective aircraft effects for 'South Pacific'.

Set Construction

'South Pacific' was the production with the biggest time demands. The cast had a long rehearsal process, and Bob Cawdle was already working on the flying rig and small rolling units for South Pacific while the set construction crew built the set for the fifth production of 1965, 'All My Sons' by Arthur Miller.

After 'All My Sons' finished, the set construction crew pitched into preparations for 'South Pacific', which included completing the rigging of half a dozen counterweighted backdrops. It is also worth noting that Bob Cawdle worked on the set construction in addition to directing '*South Pacific*'. The set construction crew worked backstage during the twenty performances, which meant that they, like the cast, were deeply involved in the production for a good many months.

Performance

We performed from Wednesday night until Sunday night four times, and I recall a sense of relief backstage during the Wednesday night of the last run of five performances because we could see the finishing line.

Then on the Thursday night, there was a tinge of sadness amongst the cast and crew because what was a great experience would soon be over. It was not just that it was a good production that made us sad that it was nearly all over; it was also that there was a good feeling amongst the cast and crew, and we were beginning to feel like professionals.

Such is the time commitment in amateur theatre. It is worth noting here that amateur means that we are not paid. It is not an indication of production standards.

'Oklahoma' 1963

Doug Jones

Doug Jones

A Spectacular Prop Goes Wrong

One of the most spectacular props used in a Repertory production was the real surrey for the 'Surrey with a Fringe on Top' scene that was used in Eleanor Williams' production of '*Oklahoma*' by Rogers and Hammerstein.

The surrey provided a brilliant background to 'Surrey with a Fringe on Top' but balanced that with being a bit of a pest backstage. Theatre 44 does not have very much wing space, and this lack of space made getting the surrey into position before and after it was used a bit of a problem. This led to a near disaster during a performance.

Just as the stage crew was finishing dragging the surrey into position to be pushed on to the stage, the front upstage wheel fell off. Stage crew members Bruce Bowden and Doug Jones were able to fit the wheel back on to the axle, but did not have time to fix it properly. They knew that the surrey was essential to the scene, so they decided to carry the front upstage part of the surrey while several other people pushed it. Bruce and Doug also hoped that a cloak of invisibility would hide them from the audience.

The scene went well, and the cloak of invisibility almost worked. The boys were spotted by one person - Eleanor Williams. El asked them after the show why they were lurking behind the surrey during the 'Surrey with a Fringe on Top' scene, but was full of praise for the way their quick thinking salvaged the scene when they explained what had happened. They were two very relieved people.

The Nuns
There were quite a few nuns based in Broken Hill in the 1960s, and they would often attend the final dress rehearsal of Rep productions. This led to an interesting situation at the final dress rehearsal for Eleanor Williams's production of '*Oklahoma*' in 1963.

Wanting to spice up the 'smoke house' scene a bit El had a picture of a topless young lady hanging on the upstage wall of the set. Stage manager, Reg Armstrong, was a bit worried about this at the final dress rehearsal as he was concerned that it would offend the nuns.

Reg therefore tore a piece of paper into the rough shape of a bra, and pinned it in the appropriate position on the picture. He need not have bothered because the biggest laugh when the curtain opened on the smoke house scene came from those wonderful nuns.

'Oklahoma' 1995

Marilyn Harris (Director/producer)

After 'Mikado', I was keen to try my hand at another production, this time as producer, musical director and artistic director. So in 1995 I began 'collecting' possible male singers for roles in 'Oklahoma'. I thought I might just have enough, but when it came to auditions the most wonderful tenor turned up, and we ended up with a black African American 'Curley'.

It is amazing where you find possible actors, and I found one of our tenants, a Torres Strait Islander who loved to sing, and cast him as Jud. He did an excellent job of the dark character who actually fires a couple of shots in the show. Unfortunately, the starter pistol most often failed to fire on cue, and the actor had to stamp on the floor or at one stage turn around and say, 'Bang'.

On a Sunday matinee, our Jud had forgotten the show was on and did not turn up. We had a packed house, with a lot of ladies from the retirement homes. So my husband, John, offered to play the part, carrying the script as he had been singing in the chorus and knew what went on. I must say he did a creditable job, but being John, who is a bit of a joker, he played the role more as a comedy and in the last scene died very dramatically three times.

Cameron Marshall was Ali Hakim, the pedlar, and got up to his usual tricks, with Barry Cosman as a perfect foil. Ali Hakim had to plead with the farmer (Barry) for his daughter's hand and, at one stage, knelt before him. Barry inserted his finger lightly in Cameron's nose and raised him to standing position. Then Cameron declared another time, 'I'm a piddler, you know', followed by Barry at the end of the scene saying, 'I still say the piddler gets my daughter'.

'Show Boat' 1967

Doug Jones

That Shotgun

There have been a few versions of the shotgun incident in Rep's 1967 production of *'Show Boat'* by Jerome Kern and Oscar Hammerstein, directed by John Barrett. I was there as part of the stage management team, and I dare to say that this is a definitive account of what happened.

There was a scene in which the two backwoodsmen were on stage, with one of them carrying a shotgun. He would prod his pal in the back with the gun and then point it upwards and fire it. The blanks which had been provided for the production gave a satisfying pop when the gun was fired, and the cardboard wad more or less crawled out of the barrel and dropped harmlessly on the floor.

One night, there was a very loud double bang when the gun was fired, and the backwoodsman who had been prodded by the gun went a strange colour. We quickly realised that the second bang was the sound of the cardboard wad going through the roof, which meant that the safety of the blanks was a problem.

Reg Armstrong immediately confiscated the rest of the blanks, and instructed that blanks for the rest of the performances be obtained from the Gun Shop, which was a reputable firearms business in Oxide Street, at Rep's expense.

There were no more holes in the roof, and the second backwoodsman was able to relax.

'Show Boat' 1967

John Curtis

The story I recall about Rep was during *'Show Boat'* performances. Two country "hicks" came to see a show with their shotguns, jeans and chequered shirts. They sat on a false stage at stage left and enjoyed the show. They got carried away and in the excitement, discharged their guns. Of course they had blanks.

One night, they pulled the trigger of one gun that was pointed skywards and a large hole appeared in the ceiling of Theatre 44. The blanks were checked more carefully thereafter!

'Show Boat' 1967

Lorraine McIntyre

Lorraine McIntyre

I have very many special memories of Rep, beginning with *'Oklahoma'* in 1963, when I played Laurie, *'Show Boat'* in 1967 and all the Rep/Harmonic productions. Wonderful times, wonderful memories!

It was *'Show Boat'* that left a real impression through an incident not going to script. In my role of Magnolia I was singing (I believe it was the reprise of 'Can't help lovin' dat man') while walking along the catwalk of the Cotton Blossom when my high heel got caught in the hem of my evening gown and brought me to an abrupt halt! I was supposed to walk down the steps at the end of the catwalk to Captain Andy (John Barrett) on the deck but could not move! However through a break in the song I was able to 'stage whisper' to John the dilemma of the heel and say, "Lift me down". Fortunately, he comprehended this unrehearsed incident, came to my aid and lifted me down to the deck where I needed to be and the show went on!

It was scary at the time, but it was a great show with great people. I have very fond memories of 'Julie' and all the cast, plus musical and stage producers.

'Show Boat' 1967

John Barrett (Director)

John Barrett

In 1967, I co-directed the musical *'Showboat'* with the late great Brian Martin.

Rehearsals went like clockwork. I have never seen a large musical production go so smoothly. You could say it was miraculous.

The time is 7.45 p.m. on opening night, curtain-up at 8.00 p.m. sharp. There am I, last minute check of the set and backstage. In storms the supposedly unflappable Brian.

'I can't handle 'em, perhaps you can - I'm at the end of my tether.'

'What?' I asked.

'Them. Them out on the verge. They're sitting out the front on the lawn'. [Yes, we had lawn out the front in the good old days, folks]. 'Hopeless! Absolutely hopeless! I'm in need of a double brandy. I'm going around the corner to the Hillside.' [Yes, we had a pub around the corner back in the good old days as well, folks.]

Out through the men's dressing room door goes I, to find our Negro cast, no make-up, with their butts stuck firmly to terra firma as scores of patrons are heading for the auditorium looking askance at a sizeable group of the '*Show Boat*' cast.

'OK, troops, what's the prob?'

Up stands their official spokesperson, 'Neville the devil'. (Little short pommy fella. Can't think of his last name for the life of me.) 'It's the makeup.'

'What's wrong with it?'

'It's greasepaint.'

'Yep, so it is. Very observant of you, Nev.'

'Well, by the time we get it off, we're always late for the after parties.'

'Is that it?'

'You don't have to scrape the stuff off. It takes forever.'

'How come this wasn't brought up or sorted out before this?'

'We asked Brian to change it a week ago.'

'Hmmm. OK, how about if you put it on for tonight and I'll get water based tomorrow.'

Our black minstrels nodded in agreement.

The opening night curtain went up twenty minutes late and our next nineteen performances went off without a hitch.

Barry Cosman and Megan Hendy (Master of the House)– Les Miserables excerpts '...in Concert' - 1996

Pop!

Doug Jones

Eugenie Bond had the slightly puzzling, as I saw it, idea that I would make an ideal butler for her 1965 production of 'The Sleeping Prince' by Terence Rattigan. I agreed to do it and found that a role with no dialogue and only requiring me to serve supper to the prince and his showgirl during a ten-minute appearance was within my acting skills. What I was not prepared for was the moment when one of those *things that makes live performance magical* happened to me.

The supper scene began with major domo (Jim Leo) opening the magnificent double doors made by Ken Arnall and leading on a little procession. Immediately behind Jim were the footmen, played by John and Laurie Camilleri, with a traymobile on which was the supper, and I brought up the rear. The supper was two bowls of easily digested jelly and custard, and there was also a bottle of champagne. Well, it was actually ginger ale decanted into a champagne bottle, firmly corked, and given a good shake as I had to pop the cork at a strategic moment before I served the supper to punctuate a remark made by the prince (played by Ken Arnall).

The traymobile was parked in an alcove at the rear centre of the set, with the major domo on one side and the footmen in their positions on either side of the double doors. I stood in front of the traymobile with my back to the audience and, as I had some time to fill in before carrying out my butler duties, kept busy by polishing the champagne glasses and cutlery without drawing the attention of the audience.

I would shift the champagne bottle during this little bit of discreet business, and this went hilariously wrong one night. As I shifted the bottle the cork popped out and hit me in the right eye, then landed in one of the desserts. I immediately cracked up rather badly, but fortunately I had my back to the audience so they would only have seen my shoulders shaking as I giggled uncontrollably.

I fished the cork out of the dessert and wiped it, re-corked the bottle, and gave it a subtle shake in the hope of having a decent POP when I opened it. Sadly, all I got was a disappointing little *phu"*. I managed to pull myself together in time to serve the supper, which I did with the poker face of all poker faces.

I then had to do one of those 'walking backwards and bowing' exits that one does when leaving the presence of royalty. As soon as I was out of view of the audience, I turned and bolted for the dressing room. Any hope I had of containing myself when I got there disappeared when I saw lighting operator Derek Denniss, doubled over and in a state of near hysterics. Derek had seen what had happened! Then the footmen came into the dressing room threatening to do bad things to me as they saw what happened, and my reaction, but as they were facing the audience they just about burst, as they struggled to avoid reacting.

The Nasty Judge

Doug Jones

Television talent quests invariably have amongst the panel of judges a nasty one whose job is to entertain by giving a contestant a verbal kicking. Some viewers enjoy this; others wince.

A nasty judge once had his moment at Theatre 44. The occasion was a one-act play festival on Queen's Birthday weekend in 1971. The format was for a performance of the three-act play 'Murder in the Cathedral' by T S Eliot as a curtain raiser on the Friday night (and was not to be judged). Then there were the one-act plays on the Saturday and Sunday afternoons and evenings. The judges for the one-act plays were a lady from Sydney and a man from Adelaide. Each of them was respected in theatre circles.

The man had an extra string to his bow; he was one of the early nasty judges in a television talent quest. He offered before the performance of 'Murder in the Cathedral' to speak to the audience about the play after the final curtain and, perhaps aware of his nasty judge reputation, gave an assurance that his comments would be low-key and constructive.

He walked on to the forestage in front of the curtain to speak to the audience after the final curtain, and the cast and stage crew were gathered behind the curtain to hear his remarks. The prompt for the play was a stenographer, and she prepared to take down the comments about the play in shorthand.

His initial remarks were indeed low-key and constructive. As he warmed up, though, he began to move backwards and forward across the forestage, and his remarks segued to those of the nasty judge. The cast was increasing distressed by the comments, the stage crew became increasingly angry, and the prompt was so angry that she was unable to continue taking shorthand notes.

The lady judge took the cast aside at the after-show party and spent some time undoing the damage.

His comments during the one-act play festival were constructive, but that did not erase the bitter memories of the opening night.

Snippets of Memory

John Pickup

John Pickup

Fifty-one years ago in 1962, Repertory presented 'The Diary of Anne Frank' by Francs Goodrich and Albert Hackett at the Police Boys' Club. I played Mr Van Daan and my main memory was walking on duckboards over ankle-deep water in the downstairs dressing room.

As Doug Jones outlined, Bob Cawdle and others worked closely with the MMA to obtain our own playhouse, opening in 1963 with Bob's 'Open House' by Philip Mackie. Since then, many outstanding productions have entertained and enthralled.

Unlike many theatre groups, Rep has survived. Fifty years later, I am personally buoyed by the fact that there is an active group of young people working in the theatre - they are the future for Repertory. They follow those gathered here who worked in the golden years of amateur theatre, before the invasion of the electronic age of computers, videos, iPhones, and the social media attractions of Facebook and Twitter.

I derived great pleasure from my association with Rep - as a producer, actor, chairman, board member - and proudly, a life member.

Best wishes to colleagues I worked with - and to the next generation who will ensure that Repertory continues for many years to come.

John Pickup, Roy Mitchell, Ken Arnall
'The Roaring Days', 1964 Written and directed by John Pickup and Roy Mitchell

Snippets of Memory

John Curtis

John Curtis

In one play, I had multiple walk-on parts. In one scene, I came in smoking an old pipe. The character on stage would look up and say, 'Good evening Captain Windy.' One night, I forgot about the walk on part, and did not change into Captain Windy's costume. The onstage character nonchalantly looked up and said, 'Good evening...[pause] .... Fred!'

Rehearsals went on for weeks prior to a show. One female actress had trouble with an important line and would always say it with the wrong emphasis. Despite being pulled up and corrected every time, she still got it wrong. In a dramatic fashion, I pretended to lose my cool - yelled at her, and stopped the final rehearsal. She broke down in tears. After a short break, we backed up and did the scene again. She got it right and did in every performance. We became good friends and still laugh together, forty-five years later, as we remember the faked anger.

Snippets of Memory

John Barrett

In the year 1965, I began what I thought at the time would be a two or three-year stint, having a bit of fun at the Broken Hill Repertory Society.

I started with some bit parts in the mid sixties, *'South Pacific'*, *'Six Months Grace'*, *'Tom Jones'*, to name a few.

The Crucible
The first lead role I jagged was that of John Proctor in a drama titled *'The Crucible'* by Arthur Miller, a period piece about the Salem witch hunts in the USA in the 1700s to 1800s.

Act 2 scene 3. Picture this - John Proctor has just returned home to his loving wife and children after a six-month jail term. It was an ultra dramatic scene, folks, as loving wife meets loving husband at the door.

The scene was flowing along swimmingly until I happened to glance over to the prompt corner to see the prompt and a couple of cast members off stage doubled over with mirth pointing in my direction.

"What's the matter with those tossers?" I wondered idly. Puzzled, I looked down, and to my utter mortification, I was confronted with a row of buttons.

Ever tried to unobtrusively do up a dozen buttons of your fly in front of an audience of approximately two hundred? Tricky!

Funeral Parlour

Now I'm not too sure of the play's name, it could have been *'Romanoff and Juliet'*, a Russian take on *'Romeo and Juliet'* written by Peter Ustinov. I *do* know that whatever the name of the production it was directed by Tom McReynolds.

As there was another production rehearsing at the theatre at that time, our cast had to find another venue to rehearse in for a couple of weeks. Now Tom was a local funeral director and had his business at the top end of Argent Street, next door to the Duke of Cornwall Hotel.

So for a month, three nights a week, we rehearsed in Tom's cellar, seated on coffins (Tom assured us they were empty, for which we were eternally grateful I can assure you), scripts in hand, and the smell of embalming fluid assailing our nostrils.

I swear, forty years on, that aroma lives with me still!

Don's Party

'Don's Party' by David Williamson was staged in 1977.

It was directed by R. Paul Brady, and I scored the part of Don, with the harrowing experience of using the dreaded *f* word on stage.

Ten minutes into act 1 scene 1 the big moment arrived. *"Aww to hell with it"*, I thought to myself. *"Let's deliver it with gusto"*.

There was deathly silence for about ten seconds - uh-oh, lead balloon time, folks.

Then the laughter came, and we never looked back for the next nine nights.

'Open House'

Doug Jones

There was a brief scene in Bob Cawdle's 1963 production of *'Open House'* by Phillip Mackie that would have been mildly amusing for the audience, but which had the stage crew and off-stage actors crowded into the stage manager's corner at every performance to listen to it.

What the audience heard was Colonel Armstrong (played by Keith Bywaters) rattling off the nicknames and surnames of a dozen or so of his old regimental colleagues to a slightly bemused-looking Harold Partridge (played by Hartley Williams). The stage crew and off-stage actors could simply not miss this little bit of *'Open House'*.

The reason was that Keith would get all the nicknames and surnames right in each performance, but kept the backstage mob entranced by randomly reshuffling them at each performance. The bemused look on Harold Partridge's face was not Hartley's acting; it was Hartley wondering where his cue line might finish up. The remarkable thing is that Keith always got the final name – and Hartley's cue – right.

Snippets of Memory

Diane Jones (Cotterill)

Diane Cotterill

During the run of '*The Sound of Music*' by Rodgers and Hammerstein (1975) the sound man, Doug Jones, fell ill with a very bad case of the flu. The result was that his wife, Diane, who was in the chorus of nuns, was running up and down the ladder to the sound booth in her very voluminous habit to play the sound effects. Luckily no cues were required at the same time she was required to be on-stage singing.

On the opening night of the show, the lead nun (June Marie Dolman/ Bennett), who was to start the whole show, was temporarily stricken by stage fright, and could not produce the required 'Dixit Dominus, Domino Meo'. After a few aborted tries, Diane jumped in and sang the lead. The musical director later commented that he was so glad *somebody* took over, or the show would never have got off the ground!

In '*Aladdin*' (1972), the person responsible for loading up the flash powder which created the effect whereby the rather substantial genie, Bob Browne, appeared was rather too generous - with the result that the effect was enhanced by the raining down of broken glass from the lights!

And in Widow Twankey's laundrette scene, the cast were required to run around and around a central grandfather clock, periodically opening the case to look inside. Cue much unscripted laughter when some wit placed inside the nude centrefold from Cleo!

And who could forget Cameron Marshall as Pooh-Bah in 'The Mikado', instructing Koko to 'mop it off' as he handed him a mop rather than a sword?

Matthew Huxtable (Ko Ko) & Cameron Marshall (Pooh Bah) 'Mikado' - 1992 directed by Marilyn Harris

Snippets of Memory

Rosemary Clarke

Bob and Rosemary Clarke

I joined Rep as soon as I arrived in Broken Hill in 1974. My first appearance was in *'Mame'* by Lawrence and Lee. In a scene where she had been out riding with Beauregard, Auntie Mame lost her skirt and was left standing there in her flesh-coloured undies as Beau said his next line, 'What a marvellous seat that woman has.' It brought the house down!

My debut as a director was *'The Anniversary'* by Bill McIlwraith. I also had to play the lead as the actress became unwell a couple of weeks before opening night. We took the play on tour to Wilcannia.

My years with Rep were wonderful. I made so many friends. I particularly enjoyed working with the teenagers over the Christmas holidays.

I really do not know how many plays I appeared in and how many I directed or worked backstage for. Rep was a huge part of my life and also of my husband Bob's, with our daughter Ann following in our footsteps.

When we did 'Pygmalion' by George Bernard Shaw, which was the forerunner of the musical 'My Fair Lady', a lot of people in the audience asked why we had left out the songs!

Snippets of Memory

Doug Jones

The Small Audience

It was a mid-week performance of one of those plays where I was persuaded to play a very small part. I was the first to exit after the play commenced and made a remark to the effect that there were very few people in the audience as I passed Reg and the techies in the corner.

My mischief continued at interval when I peeked out the men's dressing room door and remarked that *both* of the audience were outside. This got a well-deserved laugh from the mob in the dressing room!

Reg Armstrong repeated my comment when the director came backstage and was chastised for demoralising the cast. Reg very bluntly pointed out that we were not blind.

Makeup

Having make-up applied was something that all cast members had to front up to back in the good old days of Rep.

At one end there were the few minutes spent in the make-up chair by those actors who were only on stage for a short time. At the other end of the scale was the brilliant artistry of Frank Coorey's make-up of Rhiannon Jones in 'Anastasia' (1966). Rhiannon would have been around twenty at the time, and was cast as the elderly Dowager Empress of Russia.

Frank's transformation of an attractive young lady into an elderly woman took well over an hour, and those of us privileged to see him at work were in awe of his skill. Rhiannon's acting skills complemented Frank's make-up to produce a convincing portrayal of the Dowager Empress.

There were also those times when the task of the make-up people was complicated, not so much by the complexity of the makeup required but by the sheer volume of people to be done. This was the case in 'South Pacific', where one of my tasks as stage manager was to unlock the theatre soon after 6.30pm on performance nights so that the cast of around fifty could be made up in time for curtain up at 8pm.

Rep's make-up team were remarkable artists.

A Perfect Storm
This is about how my decision in 1970 to attend a summer school led to me discovering a regrettable attitude in amateur theatre.

I wanted to attend a summer school on technical theatre so that I could be a better stage manager, but the only summer schools with a theatre theme that I could track down were for amateur *actors*. Thinking that it might be fun to experience a bit of what those crazy people on stage do, I decided to attend a two week summer school at the University of New England that would be run by National Institute of Dramatic Arts (NIDA) tutors -Peter Carroll, Aubrey Mellor and Ton Witsel.

The school commenced with some very confronting exercises and improvisations that we quickly realised were intended to attack our inhibitions, but the tutors were very coy whenever we raised the "I" word. Near the end of day 2 they told us that we had just completed the first week of NIDA, to which we responded with a sardonic 'Thanks'. In response to our question, 'How did we do?' Peter said, 'Good, good, very good'. And we did too, because those two scary days converted us from thirty seriously inhibited individuals into a group of uninhibited idiots ready for whatever they threw at us.

About half-way through the first week, during a chat over a coffee, a group of us agreed that the amateur groups which we came from would be suspicious of what we were doing. This was certainly true in my case, because when I fronted up at Rep after I returned to Broken Hill, I copped some sarcastic remarks about method acting. This was ironic because we did not go near 'the method'.

The work we did was generally intended to broaden our imaginations as actors and give us confidence in ourselves as well as the ability to trust our fellow performers. Two subjects that we did that were particularly popular were 'voice' with Peter Carroll (who had speech qualifications from one of London's premier theatre schools) and 'mime' with Ton Witsel (who trained in mime with Jean- Louis Barrault, who was thought by many to be better than Marcel Marceau).

I would have preferred to have done a *techies* summer school, but I cannot deny that I enjoyed the summer school for acting. It did not make me an actor, but it was fun being an uninhibited idiot for a few weeks!

Some years later, I met Chris Ross-Smith, who set up the theatre studies faculty at UNE. When I mentioned attending a summer school at UNE Chris was keen to know which one it was, and as soon as I said, "The one in 1970 with Peter Carroll, Aubrey Mellor and Ton Witsel," Chris told me that the 1970 summer school had gone down in legend as 'The summer school of all time'.

I hope that the attitude of amateur theatre towards this type of theatre training has become more tolerant. The bottom line is that amateurs should be open to enhancing their theatre skills.

.... Amateurs!

A reliable person told me during the run of Eleanor Williams's 1963 production of 'Oklahoma!' that he heard a well known person around town say that he would not bother seeing 'Oklahoma!' because, 'They're only amateurs'.

I told the people in the dressing room before the show that night about this remark, prompting lighting guru Derrick Denniss to take a deep draw on his beloved pipe and say, 'Yes, but we're bloody good ones'.

And we were bloody good ones.

The person who called us amateurs in the derogatory sense obviously belonged to the school of thought that had everyone in amateur theatre as an unskilled idiot. There are obviously things that are done better in professional theatre simply because they are in the hands of highly skilled administrators, performers, and technicians and are much better resourced.

Amateurs should not be discouraged by this.

For a start, we should not think of amateur as a standard; it simply means that we are involved in theatre because we love it and do not care about not being paid. The important thing is that we should do those things that we *can* do as well as professional theatre and work hard to achieve a high standard in other areas.

We can, for instance, emulate professional theatre in providing a good pre show atmosphere. Our front-of-house people can be as helpful and well presented as those in professional theatre, and the foyer can be as well dressed as a foyer at a professional theatre.

In Rep's golden era, the audience was admitted to the theatre at around 7.40 p.m. The sound and lighting checks were completed by then, and everything on-stage was ready, and there was no backstage noise. There were 'warmers' on the curtains and appropriate pre show music playing, and the atmosphere was as good as that in a professional theatre because house manager Ron Herriman greeted the audience as they entered the auditorium. The actors and crew then did their best to provide excellent theatre.

Ron Herriman

'Annie Get Your Gun' (1980)

Genny Philip

Genny Philip

I first joined Theatre 44 in 1980 for the production of *'Annie Get Your Gun'*, directed by Kate Finlayson and John Barrett.

The audition was crowded and very busy with people trying out for leading roles as well as lesser roles with speaking parts, singing and dancing. I don't think anyone was turned down and although I was only interested in being in the chorus as I loved to sing, I was also chosen to be the war horse ceremonial dancer. My name became War Horse thereafter, in order to avoid confusion with the other Jennys in the cast.

Greg McMahon was chosen to play Frank Butler and a lady named June as Annie. With such demanding roles, I was very impressed with their talent as actors and singers.

With a cast of thirty-seven people, we rehearsed for three months, and the results were tremendously successful. The show played for six weeks with five performances a week, Thursday and Friday evening, Saturday matinee, Saturday evening and Sunday matinee.

The costumes were marvellous, and some cast members had more than one part. There were cowboys and Indians, a Chinaman, clowns, acrobats, dignitaries in black tie, and ladies in wonderful ball gowns. Peter Caprioli was excellent as Pawnee Bill and bore an amazing resemblance to the original.

I made a lovely traditional cream Indian dress with a brown fringe on the hem and yoke and a mock bead trim in yellow and tan. My dance costume was aqua blue with black fringe and black, red, and white mock bead trim, with matching cuffs and headband. I used these costumes for years but later donated them to the Lifeline op shop.

The direction was brilliant, but there were hiccups of course.

In one dress rehearsal, Annie's brothers and sisters from the back woods came on-stage looking as if they had just stepped out of a bath, all shining and clean. Good troupers all, after suggestions from Kate F., they next did the scene with less of a shine, hair dull and mussed, untidy clothes and smudged faces. They truly looked and acted their part.

The opening scene began with the shout, 'It's Indians! Indians!' followed by a great yelping and hollering by the cast who played Indians as they ran onstage. I wanted to play my part accurately and ran on shouting, 'hoka hey, a hoka hey! A mota meyo!' which means 'Watch out, watch out, they are going to get us.'

One night, I became confused and yelled out a greeting, 'Yatahey! Yatahey!' which was a suitable substitute, but I mispronounced it, instead turning it into the pun, 'I am good at making many babies.'

I laughed at my gaff with some relief at knowing that there would not be too many people in the audience who could speak Navajo.

Kate F. and I worked on the choreography for the ceremonial dance, which was performed before Annie's adoption into the tribe with the song 'I'm an Indian Too'.

Before the dance, in order to facilitate a scene change, I was required to stand in front of the curtains and sing a chant. I was unfamiliar with the melody from the musical score and could not read music, so I was asked if I could make up a chant. I was familiar with some genuine Dakota (Sioux) chants and warbled them. Kate was impressed, and so I sang 'One Eyed Squirrel' and 'Naming Song' in the Navajo language for each performance. A few people asked me if these were genuine Indian songs. and if so, what did they mean. I jokingly gave the translation as, 'I have an itch on my back which I can't reach. Would you mind scratching it for me?'. Somebody expressed disappointment at that, so I changed my translation to 'Oh daughter of the sun, oh daughter of the moon, you are now a daughter of the Sioux!' Who was to know?

This was sung as I stood in a strong spotlight. I then raised a staff above my head and ululated a loud war cry! (I could always play cowboys and Indians with the best of them as a child). I was then to run down a small set of steps, turn left in front of the middle row of audience chairs and out through the foyer to go backstage.

All this went off without a hitch during rehearsals, but during the first performance, which was pennies' night, the house lights were off. I was blinded by the spotlight and nearly lost my footing on the steps. I ran forward and couldn't see a thing. I had no idea where I was in the theatre. I took one more step, turned left, and collected my hip on a chair. The lady sitting in the chair gave a gasp of surprise. I stopped momentarily and recognised that strange glow from the middle row - the glint of light from the spectacles of the pensioners sitting in the audience. I regained my bearings and ran for the light in the gap between the drawn curtains separating the foyer and theatre.

I discussed this problem with Kate F, and it was decided that Rao, who was in charge of lighting, would simply turn off the spotlight after I gave the war cry. The problem was solved and never once did I land in the lap of some unsuspecting theatre patron.

Pennies' night was the last dress rehearsal of all productions. Called open night at other theatres, the public is invited to attend free of charge. This practice gives the cast members and directors audience feedback. Things may be added, deleted or changed accordingly. Theatre 44 invited the pensioners of Broken Hill to attend. We received great feedback from them. Their positive reactions lifted the cast members, and word of mouth added to positive advertising.

During one production, a young cast member asked me if I was ever nervous while performing on-stage, especially with all those people staring at me from the audience. I replied that from the stage one could not really see anybody, especially at night. All you can see is the light reflecting from the rows of eyeglasses.

It is not really them and us, I explained. It is like being in a garden at night. We know the garden is full of insects even if we cannot see them. The audience is just a separate, but magical world or dimension that adds to our energy on stage as we give of our best to them.

'Pinocchio' (1989)

Muriel Theoharidis

Muriel Theoharidis

On the second night of the pantomime *'Pinocchio'* (1989) we had a full house. Just as we were starting the first act the thunder cracked and rain came pouring down on the roof of the theatre.

At that moment a huge spider came out from behind the curtain and the people in the front rows started ooh-ing and aah-ing as it was moving across the front of the state. On stage were Peter Dowd as Giuseppe and Stacey Hendy as Pinocchio.

Without even pausing, Peter saw what the crowd was going mad about, and as he was saying his lines, he jumped on it and went about his role.

What made this funnier was that Peter was ad-libbing his lines along the way as Peter Ford, who was going to play the role, broke his leg on the Thursday before. The show was booked out all through the performances as Peter always did something to hold the people's interest, and Stacey played along with him.

'The Admirable Crichton' - 1957 - Police Boys Club directed by Brian Grosvenor

Matthew McAvaney, Stacey Hendy, Matt West, Megan Hendy, Andrew Barrett, Vanessa Hughes, Paul Tait - 'The Age of Aquarius' 1995 Directed by Megan Hendy

(Back) PaulHobson, Adam Singleton, Matt Bell, (Front) Bob Clarke, Jacqui Passlow, Steven Nancarrow
'Jack and the Beanstalk' 1997 Directed by Rosemary Clarke

Cast - 'The King and I' – 1980 Directed by Marge Collison

June Marie Bennett as Gairy Fodmother (Rindercella
'....in Concert' 1996

Life Members at 50th Anniversary of Theatre 44 (2013) - Airlie Pedlar, Dick Kelly, Kay McLachlan, Ann Gordon, John Barrett (back) Don Mudie, Camille Jenkins, June Marie Bennett, Megan Hendy, (seated) Eleanor Williams

Snippets of Memory

June Bennett (Dolman/Langford)OAM

June Bennett

As June Marie Dolman, my life with the local Repertory commenced in November, 1961. I was asked to be an usher and the show actually took place at the Police Boys' Youth Centre Auditorium. This was an exciting new experience, and I wanted more involvement as long as it had the elements of musical shows because of my love of music.

As June Marie Langford in July 1965, I saw auditions were open for a cast in the musical 'South Pacific' by Rodgers and Hammerstein. I became an American nurse with the group singing 'I'm Gonna Wash That Man right Outta My Hair' and other scenes. This was a huge fully costumed production requiring several main characters, chorus of male and female sailors and nurses with choreographed of dancers, and live orchestral backing.

There were many months of rehearsals and because of complexities of direction, leadership changed with Robert (Bob) Cawdle at the helm. These were the days before television, and there were twenty-one performances in November with constant packed audiences. This production was professionally executed and comparable to the movie. (Before this production, I had a baby girl, Paula, who turned one year old near the performance times. And two years later in the same month, my twin boys were born, so these years were hectic at home).

During the 1970s and 1980s, there was a feast of musical shows. I was in the chorus of singers for 'Annie Get Your Gun' in 1981 in which my children, Paula, Glenn and Bradley Langford were child extras.

In 1976 'The Pajama Game' musical was staged. One scene that was never forgotten was whilst off-stage I needed to make a quick dash to the toilet. I was the secretary and Peter Forde was my boss. Peter was on-stage talking and I was supposed to respond to his conversation. However, I was not on-stage, and he had to ad lib, walking about stage until I ran in with my lines! In other words, never presume it will be the same each performance, because things happen differently each time!

In 1977 Repertory decided to do something different, and presented an old time music hall. With master of ceremonies, Bob Clarke, and individual performers, the show was staged at three different Clubs, over three Saturday nights. The performers would choose their own acts. I was always fascinated with Carmen Miranda, a happy South American movie star who wore fruit on her head singing 'I Yi Yi Yi (I Like You Very Much'). This proved to be a favourite with the audiences and years later I still get requests for Carmen.

During 1979 a full production of 'Oliver' by Lionel Bart was staged. I had a character role as the housekeeper and my children were also involved. In 1975 a fully costumed production of 'The Sound of Music' by Rodgers and Hammerstein was mounted. It was a beautiful story and we were singing with professional-looking scenery. I was a nun and sang at the opening (as in the film). My daughter, Paula, was one of the von Trapp children.

Rep-Harmonic was formed because Repertory had the actors and Philharmonic had the singers. Nessie Osten was the musical director of three productions, each time fully costumed, all staged at the Entertainment Centre with two performances each production, and accompanied by the Broken Hill Civic Orchestra. I was in the chorus of 'Fiddler on the Roof' by Bock and Harnick in 1987 and was leading lady, Dolly, in 'Hello Dolly' by Jerry Herman in 1988, which was challenging because Dolly appeared almost in every scene. The third production, 'Carousel' by Rodgers and Hammerstein, directed by Muriel Theo and me, was staged in May, 1989 with John Bennett part of back stage crew. [June and John married the following October, 1989].

Now as June Marie Bennett, I enjoyed Muriel Theo's beautifully staged fully costumed production 'Show Boat' by Jerome Kern and Oscar Hammerstein in 1994. This was another popular choice and I was in the chorus. As a director, Muriel also did other concerts where various performers presented their solo or duet talents and I as a soloist sang Irish songs.

In another show in the 1990's, an 'Old Time Music Hall', Muriel Theo was the producer/director of what was actually a variety concert. It was easier for the performers. They could rehearse and learn their own song at home and get together for final rehearsals.

We all had a programme, and Valerie Harris and I were doing an Irish bracket in Irish costume, and we were about number 14 on the programme. I said to Val that we did not need to be there at the commencement of the show and that we would arrive in time to change for our act.

Muriel was seated in the front row to watch each of the five performance nights, and she also compered the acts using a microphone. The backstage crew was just the curtain person, with the performers, being adults (supposedly), responsible for being dressed and ready at the side of the stage. Performers followed a backstage programme in number sequence.

When Muriel announced Val and me, the curtains opened and lo and behold, it was a very blank stage. We were not in the building! Muriel, of course, was furious, and said to close the curtains. June Marie was not to know that two performers did not turn up due to sickness, and of course this changes the timing of the show. When Val and I did perform, I made up an extra skit of how two Irish colleens got lost along the Barrier Highway, which was humorous for the audience - but not with Muriel!.

Marilyn Harris as director presented several variety shows and I remember being a fairy godmother in one of her shows. In the early 1990s John and I were asked to become board members. John assisted with maintenance work and in clearing a great deal of weeds at the front, side, and back of the building.

Times had changed. Television was well established, and now a new mobile video delivery van business opened in Broken Hill. People were happy to hire the movie videos and stay at home. Furthermore, the drama plays were diminishing, with no one volunteering to be producers and directors. Theatre 44 needed upgrading, particularly with lighting and sound.

A well known past member at a board meeting felt Repertory days were over, and suggested to all present that they should vote to permanently close Theatre 44. Muriel Theo and I were horrified and said, "No!". The two of us guaranteed we could keep the theatre operative, put on a variety show and draw the public back to the theatre. With front page publicity in the *Barrier Daily Truth*, and interviews on radio, auditions and rehearsals took place and in 2004 'Save Theatre 44 Variety Show' was staged. Yes, the public returned, all seats were taken, and many people very much supported Broken Hill Repertory. I continued to support Repertory as a board member for several years.

In July, 2005, I was awarded a life membership certificate, with chairperson, Matt Palmer and secretary, Sanny Dougherty which was worded 'To commemorate a long and dedicated involvement with Theatre 44. June has performed, produced and supported musicals and dramas in the Theatre since 1961'. I still take a keen interest with this Society and attend the annual general meetings.

Barrier Daily Truth dated 8th March, 2005, stated "Life membership was bestowed upon June Marie Bennett, who began with the theatre in 1961. It is entirely befitting that in her forty-fourth year with Theatre 44, June was granted this honour for her outstanding work and support.' To Broken Hill Repertory Society I say 'Thank you for the music'. 'June is bustin' out all over!'

[Edit. June is now best known as Shirl in the movie '*Priscilla, Queen of the Desert*']

Snippets of Memory

Marilyn Harris

Marilyn Harris

I first began with Rep playing the piano for Muriel Theo's productions.

One night, Jeffery Fitzsimmons was playing the piano, and I was playing a keyboard which faced side-on to the audience. The next song, which Jeffery was to play, was 'The Sound of Music' to be sung by Alison Forner. I looked over to the side of the stage and Muriel was there around the curtain pointing to me and indicating that Alison was not there and I was to sing the song. After a little anxiety about remembering the words I started to sing the verse 'My day in the hills has come to an end I know.....' etc. When I came to the end of the verse the curtains opened and Alison sang 'The hills are alive with the sound of music.'Perfect timing. She had gone home to feed her baby and was late getting back for her cue.

Alison Forner

Accidents

1. At rehearsal I backed up across the trapdoor, tripped up, and showed everything to the boys in the audience.

2. Another rehearsal as director I fell backwards down the steps at the side of the stage.

3. In the process of letting someone in to pick up some equipment I entered through the dressing room door and found someone had removed the stairs from the stage to the audience. Rather than bother turning on all the lights, I found my way to the street side of the stage where I thought there were some steps, took a step and landed on the ground, hitting my head on the wall as I fell.

   My first thought as a first-aid-trained person was, 'Am I still conscious?' Then the pain of a broken shoulder took over. I screamed 'help' and the man who was waiting outside came on to the stage but could not see me in the dark. 'I'm here', I whimpered. 'Can you bring me my bag with my mobile phone?' We rang the ambulance, and my husband, and the man opened the front door.

   I was really uncomfortable and longed to lie down, but was thinking I would get my white clothes dirty. Silly girl. The ambulance, after a long while, went roaring by - they had been given Creedon Street as the nearest cross street. After a trip to Adelaide for an operation to insert some pins, I was OK.

4. At a Philharmonic concert at Theatre 44 in 2015 it was very cold, so some heaters were used on stage where the choir was seated. I had plugged the extension leads into the dressing room power points because I judged them to be safest. About half-way through the concert, someone looked up and pointed at the junction in the electrical lead which was on fire. Luckily I knew just where it was plugged in, so I ran down and turned it off. Apart from a little smoke and fumes, the audience was none the wiser.

Snippets of Memory

Megan Hendy (Pollard)

Megan Hendy

My first experience at Rep was as a chorus member in the pantomime 'Cinderella' by Crocker and Gilder in 1970. I had one line, 'Here he comes now, Your Highness', and I could never say it with the right inflection. Hopefully, I have improved since then!

Next, I was Rosalys, a handmaiden to Snow White, in 'Snow White and the Seven Dwarfs' in 1974. I could not have played Snow White; the dwarfs were all taller than I! That was the first year that I was in the Christmas pageant on the Rep float. I remember taking about six hours to get ready that day as I wanted everything to be perfect. I am crying in all my photos after the final performance because it was such a wonderful experience and I was devastated that it was all over.

My first 'big' role was as 'Mole' in 'Toad of Toad Hall' by A A Milne.

I thought I was so important, acting opposite three adults playing Toad, Ratty and Badger.

I was the evil fairy in *'Sleeping Beauty'*. I decided to be purple and had to paint myself before every performance. It got everywhere, took hours to get off, and took weeks to wear off completely.

In another pantomime, *'Babes in the Woods'* (1991), I played Ruggablugg and was dressed in several layers as I believe the panto was set in winter. Of course, it was the middle of summer in Broken Hill. We had a chase scene through the theatre and it was so hot, I nearly passed out and had to be sponged down in the dressing room between scenes. (Edit. I remember Megan collapsing at the side of the stage and everyone fanning her. Megan's mother, Pauline Hendy, made a lot of the costumes, which were amazing.)

In *'Oklahoma'* (1995), I was Ado Annie and had a duet with Matt West, who played Will. Part way through the song, I had to start the next verse when I went completely blank and could not remember a single word. So, for some reason, I decided to make up a dance instead. The look on Matt's face was priceless!

Speaking of dancing, I was cast in *'Show Boat'* (1994) as one-half of the dancing duo on the showboat. How I was ever cast as a dancer still amazes me. Suffice to say, it was the first and last time! I did manage to do some high kicks in very high heels though!

The highlight of my year used to be the One Act Play Festival. I loved going to Mildura to perform, even staying on a houseboat one time. Rep became my second home. I spent so many hours at the theatre, I don't know why I bothered to pay rent or buy a house!

I remember when *'Love is Contagious'* by Patricia McLain turned into *'Herpes is Contagious'* when either I or Matthew Huxtable got a cold sore.

Then there was the struggle we had getting the madrigal together in *'The Mikado'* (1992); and how Bert Henry wrote his lines in chalk on the stage and we 'three little maids' shuffled them all off.

I remember the pants my mum made for Cameron Marshall for *'The Mikado'*. He could have done the splits in them and no-one would have noticed. Cameron was a very funny man.

I decided in one show to sing 'Otto Titsling' from *'Beaches'*. It was a classic, because I was completely flat throughout the whole song! That was mainly because we had no sheet music and Marilyn, who was trying to accompany me, did not know the song.

Megan Hendy, John Barrett & Matthew Huxtable in 'Babes in the Wood' 1991 directed by Muriel Theo

"The Mikado" 1992

Marilyn Harris (Director)

In 1992, I was invited to do artistic direction for a Rep-Harmonic production of Gilbert and Sullivan's 'The Mikado'. It was my first major musical as a director, and I was privileged to have the assistance of Matthew Huxtable, who designed and painted the scenery (design based on willow pattern), played the part of Ko-Ko, and generally came up with so many ideas as assistant director.

It has always been difficult to cast male lead singers, and we could not find a Nanki-Poo in Broken Hill. One of my pupils, Corey Page, had gone to a university in Adelaide to study drama. He was a very keen actor and had a fine voice, albeit a baritone (Nanki-Poo is a tenor role). I asked him if he could learn the part in Adelaide and come up for rehearsals, and he agreed. It was a giant gamble that could have gone so wrong. However, I had faith in Corey's commitment and ability.

I sent the script and recorded songs to Corey, and he faithfully learned it all as best he could. He was to come back to Broken Hill three weeks before the first performance, and we hoped to get some good rehearsals in. As it turned out, he was delayed in Adelaide, so the rehearsal time became shorter and shorter, until Corey finally turned up on the day of the final dress rehearsal. The ever-faithful Matthew guided him through the blocking and we rehearsed as best we could, and the dress rehearsal went on as planned. The final product was better than everyone expected.

Another character in '*The Mikado*' was Cameron Marshall, who was the local manager of ABC Radio. He played an hilarious Pooh-Bah (Lord High Everything Else). When we started rehearsals we could not hear him speak until I sidled up to him and said, 'Cameron, you are using your radio voice. Can you please use your stage voice?' He was very well heard after that.

Bert Henry, Stacey Hendy, Corey Page, Alison Forner, Diane Magor-Jones, Megan Hendy and chorus from BH Philharmonic Society - 'Mikado' 1992 (RepHarmonic) Set designed and painted by Matthew Huxtable

My recollections of 'The Mikado'

Corey Page

Corey Page

One of my favourite memories related to Theatre 44 would have been when I moved to Adelaide to attend Flinders University to study drama. I was staying on campus at the time, living and breathing university life, becoming an actor, and preparing myself for the long road ahead.

It would have been half-way through my first year when I was contacted by Marilyn Harris, who played a pivotal role in my being accepted into the Flinders drama program. Marilyn was my singing/vocal coach and friend from my home town of Broken Hill. Marilyn had just started casting for a production of 'The Mikado', and was hoping that I would play the role of Nanki-Poo.

There was one big problem - I was now living in Adelaide, a six hour drive from the Silver City. It was impossible for me to attend rehearsals. How I would learn the songs and dance numbers seemed a little out of reach - 'seemed'. But Marilyn had a plan; I would learn the songs by correspondence. Marilyn would record the songs on tape at her home in Broken Hill and send them to me in Adelaide. It was the perfect solution, maybe. Over the next few weeks I would receive packages from Marilyn, the manuscript, those precious little tapes, and the encouragement that we could get through it.

The weeks rolled by, and I tucked myself away in the little music room that was on campus, to infuse myself with 'The Mikado' and Nanki-Poo. I had my doubts that it was going to work, with the performance date closing in fast and my panic rising that it would not all come together. I strained to grasp how I would learn the choreography for the dance numbers.

It was now summer, and I had bought my bus ticket to head back to Broken Hill to spend the Christmas break with my family, and, yes, to perform 'The Mikado'. The bus ride from Adelaide to Broken Hill in the middle of summer is one of the great joys of the southern hemisphere. If you have ever done it you know exactly what I am talking about; the Great Ocean Drive it is not.

When the bus rolled into Broken Hill, my mother was there to greet me, and so too was Marilyn, ready to whisk me away to get started on the dance numbers.

We had about three rehearsals before the show went up. It was a little tense with some of the other actors in the show. I will not mention any names other than Matthew Huxtable, who, although I am sure was a little put out with the audacity of the situation (how dare I assume to come in off the bus literally and perform anything with only three rehearsals), led and supported me through the rehearsals. Of course, his attitude only fuelled my desire more to do a great job for Marilyn.

All's well that ends well. Marilyn and I did do a great job. Marilyn's plan had worked, those little white tapes paid off. 'The Mikado' went off without a hitch. Well that's how I remember it. Thank you, Marilyn Harris.

[Editor's comment - Not long after this, Corey was picked up as one of the stars of the TV series "*Heartbreak High*" and is now acting in USA.]

Snippets of Memory

Matthew Huxtable

Matthew Huxtable

The first theatre I ever went into was Theatre 44. I was small, and my mother took me to a summer matinee of *'Snow White and the Seven Dwarfs'*. I recall almost nothing of the show, but I distinctly remember the theatre itself. I remember the tiny brick shed foyer and the ticket counter that had been a drinks bar in a previous life. Passing through the curtains, I remember the corrugated warehouse auditorium and the musty flippy cinema chairs that you couldn't help but pick at. But most of all, with no air conditioning and being a typical Broken Hill summer's day, I remember it being stiflingly hot.

We sat in the front section; it might have been the front row. The stage was a good height above me, so I had to sit with my head arched back looking up. But as I said, the only thing I recall of the show itself is the character Grumpy, maybe because the actress looked like she was enjoying playing the curmudgeon. Many years later, I would be partnered with that actress as everything from evil partners-in-crime to bickering roommates-cum-lovers to a married Vaudevillian act. We even flatted together for a short period before I left for university. Unfortunately we did not part well.

It was 1987. My parents saw a classified advertisement in the paper calling for young actors, and they urged me to audition. I went along and was lucky enough to get a part in the play! I was to play a helicopter.

I was done up in a cardboard box held up with braces, a propeller hat, and roller skates. I could not skate. Someone would shove me on from the wings. I would say my line while trying to keep balanced, then someone else would catch me on the other side. Hey, it's show-biz! I was very naive and very immature: once I laughed at the superstition of 'Macbeth' and was ordered to go out, spit and turn round. The next rehearsal, one of the actors tripped and sprained his ankle. The director blamed me.

My first major role would be a year later playing Charlie in 'Charlie and the Chocolate Factory' by Roald Dahl. I was still very immature, but perhaps a teeny weeny bit less naive, having had my first taste of limelight. From then on I was pretty much involved in everything, be it onstage or the back of it. Even if I wasn't needed for a production, I would still show up and sit backstage and watch.

For some unknown crazy reason, during the summer of 1991-92, I was trusted with a set of keys to the theatre. There was a gang of us youths with a theatrical bent and we used to meet every Sunday under the belief that we were developing a new group-written masterpiece. In truth, we mostly played music and mucked about. Every now and then one of us would come over all-serious, and insist that we 'workshop' an idea or 'improv' a situation. I'm pretty sure we wrote something at sometime: we did once emcee a Theatre 44 Christmas party awards night, performing little skits and miming to songs. One of the lasses and I did a Play-School inspired routine based around the 'Queen of Pop' Madonna; we thought we were comedy gold!

But of that summer's great yet-to-be-written masterpiece, nothing came of it, of course, and often those afternoons ended with us sitting on the stage around a tub of ice cream, each with a spoon. However, looking back, those wasted afternoons were my fondest memories of my time in Broken Hill. In that theatre space, we were allowed to be imaginative, to think creatively, and to play. But most of all, I got to spend time with people I liked, and whom I think also liked me. At Theatre 44 I was with friends.

It was always fun to go a little overboard on stage, to play something exaggeratedly, and pantomimes were the perfect opportunity to let rip. Surprisingly, I only performed in one panto, *'Babes in the Wood'* (1992), and I played Slinky, the evil side-kick to the now grown-up Grumpy. The music director, a genius with a Janome, had sewn me this splendid puffy-sleeved Elizabethan jacket (god, it was beautiful) and I matched it with red tights and pointy buckle shoes. At the first dress rehearsal, I wore underneath a red leopard-print G-string that I thought would flash hilariously as I bounced across the stage doing my best Paul Lynde impersonation. The music director, viewing from her position down in the pit, pulled me aside at break for a quiet word. I wore red bloomers after that.

I did all the musicals. The endless music hall hack-jobs were somewhat tedious but a necessary funding source, and I sensed that the cast and crew enjoyed themselves more than the audience did watching. (I did one dressed in a giant teddy bear costume in which I could only partly see out of one eye; I would get about the stage by counting my steps).

I was in three of the combined Philharmonic/Repertory productions, and played Ko-Ko in *'The Mikado'* (1993). I immensely enjoyed that show, though, to be honest, we'd nicked a lot of ideas from a recently televised Opera Australia production. I also designed and painted the set. It was two huge blue willow patterned backdrops with giant imperial dragons front stage, and black-framed doors covered in baking paper. I thought it looked splendid in its primary colours. Photos of that set and others, plus illustrations from many program covers, appeared in my university application design portfolio.

My last show was in January 1995, my production of 'Cinderella'. I was proud of *'Cinderella'*, though in hindsight, I wasn't a very good director and the set never looked exactly what I had imagined in my mind's eye. But still it was a fun swan song. Around lunch on opening afternoon (a panto, remember) I was taking pictures of the set. Trying to get the full set in the shot, I stepped back into nothingness and fell off the stage. I sprained my arm trying to deflect my fall and was given morphine and taken to the hospital in an ambulance. Unfortunately, I was also working on the show's sound, and had to quickly explain my notes and which cassette was which. I wasn't seriously hurt and was back at the theatre by interval. Everyone was frantic – 'Matthew this happened' and 'Matthew that happened' – but I, in my morphine state, simply hugged everyone and told them all how much I loved them.

When I left, I may have been less immature but I was definitely no longer naive to the magic of theatre. Over twenty years later, I still get goose bumps when the auditorium lights go down and the stage lights go up, eager to be part of the great pretend of the proscenium wall. That is my favourite thing about theatre: that unspoken agreement that the audience truly believes that the actors *are* struggling 1960's New York artists or Lord High Executioners or giant fairground animatronic teddy bears. I relish knowing that though a show may run for dozens of performances, each night will be ever so slightly different, the audience and the actors sharing a unique interaction that can never be experienced again. My time at Theatre 44 welcomed me into this beautiful world.

I do not act any more, which is a shame, yet I go and see as much as I can, be it tiny fifty-seater experimentals or the touring Broadway spectaculars (honestly, the tiny shows are better). I thank Theatre 44 and all those who trusted me and gave me those first opportunities to be part of a team. You gave me the greatest gift.

Matthew Huxtable as Ko Ko in 'Mikado' 1992 (background Andrew and Glendon Harris)

Rehearsal Problems

Marilyn Harris

I had enjoyed directing 'The Mikado' so much that I decided to get some kids together in the Christmas holidays and put another variety show together called 'Join the Circus'. It was January and very hot at the theatre, and then the power went off for several weeks until the problem was diagnosed and a new power pole was installed. During this time, we rehearsed in the semi-dark in an extremely hot theatre. One of the things we did to cope with the heat was to bring spray bottles and spray one another with water. You cannot keep kids down.

Snippets of Memory

Adrian (Aj) Bartley

Adrian Bartley

'Sweeney Todd' by Stephen Sondheim -1989

My first ever show; I was a shy and decidedly unsocial eighteen-year-old. I was introduced to Theatre 44 by my cousin Nathan, who with his group of friends had found themselves attracted to the idea of showing off in public! (The idea of getting laughs and applause also appealed!) Nathan thought that being involved would help me make friends and come out of my shell.

So on that day, I sat in the back row of the auditorium and just watched rehearsals happen! It was amazing to watch, so the next time, I came by myself. I was asked to help back-stage and was put under the tutelage of Jack, the stage manager. I was still a basket case and unable to talk to anyone, but I watched it all and took in everything!

My biggest memory of 'Sweeney' is, not surprisingly, of my cousin Nathan and his friends on the last night during a scene in the courtroom. A boy named Michael (age sixteen, one of the 'group') was in the role of the court guard, and had to call Sweeney Todd to the witness box. On all the other shows he called out 'Sweeney Todd, Sweeney Todd' as required. But on that final night the 'group' had to have fun, so he was instructed to only 'mouth' the words silently as he stood against the fabric flat. Behind the flat were two of the others - Zac W and Darren J - fully ready to actually call out his lines as he mouthed them.

The cue was given, and the boys were ready. The first 'Sweeney' was in a high pitched Mickey Mouse voice; the second was in a gruff comical bass and I just stood and watched as the two behind the flat scrambled to hide as Jack was heard running.

Everyone from the group was reprimanded, but the joke had happened - too late to stop. Also when Richard (playing the judge) opened his ledger on the final night, he was to find that it had been filled with, shall we say, eye-opening images cut from certain magazines!

I was not out of my shell yet, but I could see the light at the end of the tunnel! It was during interval in the dressing room one night that I was asked by John Barrett if I would like to be on-stage. I responded, 'I don't think I could, I'd be awful.' But John simply said, 'You will never know until you try.' He said that he was about to direct a play called 'My Three Angels' by Samuel and Bella Spewack and that there was a tiny role for a young guy. Against my better judgement, I agreed.

'My Three Angels'
To be honest, I do not have a lot of memories about this one - aside from sitting in the foyer with Lissy and chatting, being paranoid about remembering my handful of lines. But there is one rock solid

memory, and that is of my left leg shaking every. damn. night, from the second I stood offstage to walk on until the lights went down. It was so bad that I had to put foam on the heel of my shoe to stop the staccato backing track. I ended the play sitting centre front stage on a chair, - and that leg went nuts!

After this show was the real love of Theatre 44 - the Saturday workshops with Genny Philip. We would all turn up in the morning and stay all day, doing improvs and just chatting, laughing and realising our tribe was valid! Me, Mel, Brad C., Paddy D., Corey P. and Matthew H., - along with our den mother of 'Be weird, talk crap, have fun, live life' Genny P and her daughter Katy.

Without Genny and her 'not like the other adults' outlook, I doubt many of us would have ever become who we are! She opened our minds by laughing with us, letting us run wild with oddness, and opening her house afterwards, where we would all sit and laugh until the sun came up. There were no expectations and no structure - just creativity. And now look at us - look at me!

Every weekend, we all lived in one another's pockets, if not at Rep then on the stage in the park joking, dancing, and playing! Or we would be at Mel's house watching every daggy film you can imagine!

I could write so much about our exploits in the 'workshop'; enough to fill a lot of pages. But this is about Rep alone, so back to Rep. But those workshops were where I started to be me!

The next show was 'Little Women' by Louisa May Alcott (1990) which I had nothing to do with aside from seeing it twice - ostensibly to all hang out together.

At the end of the year was 'Aladdin' - a pantomime - and by definition 'chaotic', as it involved not only our 'workshop' gang but the 'group' of younger kids....all anarchic and all big personalities. Hold on to the seats! I was only in the chorus as were most of us, though some had leads. Amongst the many anecdotes, the one that most stood out was the Chinese laundry scene, pulling a pair of men's underpants over Lissy's head whilst in the background centre stage. Let us just say that was the only joke that can be shared!

Shortly after *Aladdin* closed, came one of the most formative performance events of my life - the '1990 Rep Xmas Party'. The order went out that everyone should come up with an 'act' to entertain all the casts, directors and patrons prior to the awards being given. There were singers, comedy acts, and dramatic readings.

Basically we, 'Zac's group and the workshop kids,' saw it as the only chance we would get to do stuff on stage that Rep in its relatively staid attitude would allow, so the comedy was raunchy. There was *Monty Python* and some solid monologues - and my bit!

We knew 100 per cent that Rep would never do *'Rocky Horror'* but it was our mantra. We watched it almost every week, and we sang along. It was about weirdos and freaks, not fitting in and being yourself. So we came up with the idea to do a track from the show, but it had to be secret by definition, a 'show-stopper'.

So we cast it:- Lissy as Janet, Huxy as Brad, Corey as Riff Raff, Mel as Columbia, Paddy as Eddie, Brad as Rocky -The sight gag was too good to pass up (we shoehorned him into a 5 year-old's leopard print leotard!) - and me as Frank.

No one knew I could dance; I had never done it in public. I had started teaching myself in 1984 as a way of controlling something amongst the bullying and loneliness. I would watch clips and practice while Mum was at the pub. It was the only thing I had faith in, and it was my biggest secret! But Mel had seen me do some stuff and was impressed, and ever since I had seen *'The Rocky Horror Picture*

Show' in 1984 I had been in awe of Frank. He was who I wanted to be - confident, powerful and freaky!

So I was Frank for a few weeks! We spent a few weeks secretly rehearsing in Mel's back-yard. She choreographed Brad, Corey, and Paddy into the back row and I was left to make it up as I went. Lissy and Huxy did not need all the rehearsal as they would be 'warm props' and only there for me to dance around and play with on-stage, so they only came in on the last rehearsal!. We made costumes, corsets and capes and hit op shops for tail coats and pencil skirts. Mel's mum took apart an old dress and made my lace gloves and wrap. I hacked the legs off a pair of women's Corfu jeans to make hot pants - until it was decided they were not short enough, and they were cut even higher - scary high! We sewed, laughed, and watched RHPS non-stop!

The boys, though, had never seen me dance. I had never danced in front of anyone, and Corey was concerned if I had the ability and confidence. He was not alone; I did not know either!

We told no one outside the cast because we were scared that someone would object! The only 'adults' who knew were Mel's mum and Genny who would be doing my make-up, based not on Tim Curry but a vintage 'Boy George' image.

Two days before the party, we finally rehearsed on the Theatre 44 stage. We grabbed an old box as Frank's throne and threw fabric over it. We threw bright tulle over the Aladdin set and waited for Lissy and Huxy to arrive. Then we ran it - I just walked it and mimed. I still had no idea what I was gonna do.

Once the song was over the first time, Lissy became withdrawn and visibly upset. She was younger than us, and her background was a bit more conservative. She was actually shocked by the song content, never having seen the film. She called her mum to pick her up and pulled out.

With only one day to go, we called our school friend, Lyndle C., to step in as Janet. She turned up and we ran it again. After two run-throughs, as we were stepping down those notoriously awful steps at the end of the runway, Lyndle fell and badly twisted her ankle. We were not having much luck with our Janets. But Lyndle was, and is, a trooper, so she powered on and would still be Janet.

But all the running from Frank and being pushed around and 'played with' were out. So she and Huxy would come on *stage right* in front of the curtain and stand watching. In their section, Huxy would help her across the stage and back and I would have to not physically interact. (We lost some amazing stuff - but the show has to go on)

Party night. We all arrived an hour early and Genny and I went straight to work on the make-up (after spraying my hair with three cans of black hairspray!). When I was painted, I hid. I climbed up into the loft and sat there in hotpants, corset and full face make-up! People started arriving and were told that I was not able to be there. I was in the loft for almost two hours and then it was 'DEFCON 5' as we all scrambled to get ready. Mel threw on her Lurex mini that we had hacked with scissors and sewn tulle on and threw on some extreme make-up. Corey vanished and dressed as Riff Raff. Paddy was already wearing his jeans and white shirt, so he was lookout! And Brad went up into the sound booth with the RHPS cassette and cued it up.

When all was clear, I climbed down, grabbed a black-painted backdrop and draped it as my cape. Then I rushed out to the foyer (hoping like hell the doors were not locked!)

Nathan had been instructed to sit at the end of the cat-walk and film 'the last skit' and was told that Huxy and Lyndle getting on-stage was the cue. No one knew anything!

Brad hit 'Play' and we were off. And I still had <u>no idea</u> what I was gonna do! I knew my stage moves 'To chair, drop cape, move forward, move back etc', but had <u>no</u> idea about the actual dancing. Scary!

The next four minutes were a blur. Music started, and I walked in and up onto the catwalk. The cape was heavy and awkward, but I had to keep moving and keep my face mobile. I felt stupid in the Brad and Janet bit because I could only stand there as opposed to the planned routine. The plastic glass I was holding was thrown and broke onstage. But aside from that the video existed, and people reacted, were shocked and laughed!

You can hear it all on the video! Afterwards we were applauded, and John talked about trying to actually do the show. Muriel wanted me to dress as Cher for her next music hall, and we all ended up on the stage in the park in full makeup until sunrise. That's the night I realised what I could do.

(Also since that day I have <u>never,</u> not even once, had stage fright - no more shaky legs - cos I actually knew in my soul - It's what I do!)

After that, I went back to high school after being kicked out three years prior. I had decided that I could actually do it. But it meant that Rep had to take a back seat. The 'Saturday workshops' died off as we all were at school together and constantly together. I was in a few more actual plays. '*Love Is Contagious*' is the most memorable as that is where I met a lady who was to become a lifelong friend - Megan Hendy.

The only things I could/would commit to were music halls or small roles that required minimal rehearsal as I had promised myself I was going to do well at school, and my social life had exploded. Rep was the launch-pad.

I was in another panto in 1991 'Babes in the Woods,' cast as The Demon Alcohol and I was thrilled. It was my chance to really play operatic nasty and to do full make-up and performance. I was so happy.

But then the actor who had a large supporting role as Will Scarlet got glandular fever and could not fulfil the role. I was asked to play his role as well, so goodbye make-up and theatrics, and hello stupid mask and ludicrously quick change. But he was ill, a friend and these things happen.

It also meant that I had to sing on-stage which was then, and is still my Achilles heel. I am not confident singing at all. But it was one simple song 'Red Red Robin,' and another more comical routine about wallpapering a parlour that I mimed and/or mumbled while making sure to prat-fall to hide it all!

Honestly, as annoyed as I was to lose the fun of the villain role - I was OK with helping out my friend and the production - at first. And this is my main reminiscence about that show - and I'm still angry.

On the second Saturday night and into the Zen groove of the dual role, quick change and my routine, said friend came in and said that his family were in the audience that night, and he was OK to play Will - twenty minutes before curtain! I was surprised but said, 'Yeah, OK.'. So I added to the Demon makeup and went on! I was annoyed, but OK.

The next day before the Sunday matinee, I spent an hour doing detailed make-up for the Demon, as I assumed the friend was now obviously OK to play his role. Nope! Ten minutes before curtain he wandered in and said, 'Nah I'm still not well enough' and went to sit and chat. So I had to do the quick change (literally run in cloak from foyer, get fully out of make-up, wig etc and into Scarlett costume and on-stage in three minutes) but this time with a full face of make-up.

Long story short, I took the laboured-over make-up off straight away, put the dopey mask on and did the show - then left! No way was I able to go to the party. (It took a good few weeks before I could look the now former friend in the eye - and to this day it still makes my blood boil!)

But one golden comedy moment in that show was when while during a typical 'comical chase through audience' panto scene, a long time patron became <u>very</u> involved and actually grabbed the lead child and happily screamed, 'Matt, Matt I got her for ya'. The said child's theatrical, 'Oh help me, help me' quickly changed to a blood curdling scream. Ahhh panto! Gotta love it!

At some point in this period, I was involved in a 'music hall' and did a dance routine. Because of school, I said I would only be involved on the two Saturday night shows, and as is my wont, I did not rehearse. Heck, I couldn't even be bothered choosing between the three songs to dance to, so I cued up the three songs on separate cassettes and at interval wandered in to the dressing room and gave the tapes to the sound man, and said, 'Pick one'. He was a little concerned at this but I loved it. The <u>only</u> thing I was ever confident about was my dancing and ability to freestyle, so not knowing what song I was going to perform until I heard it start on stage thrilled me! Hearing the opening refrain of Malcolm McLaren's 'Deep in Vogue' still takes me straight back there!

Since I was avoiding large commitments (plays) there were a few other music halls. I sang - badly, but I had to face that demon - songs from 'Barnum', I played a bra thief in the song Otto Titsling from 'Beaches' sung by Megan Hendy, but that was it.

Until I was ready to leave Broken Hill in early 1994. My friend Megan was to direct 'Beauty and the Beast' and asked me to audition. I said no as I planned to move to Geelong in early January, but I attended the auditions as moral support. At the time there were some personal issues; and as a result I realised that helping out with *B&B* would be the right thing to do.

Somehow I got the lead, and finally my chance to do make-up on stage. So I delayed my moving to Victoria until the play was over. (I actually left town two days after the final matinee) I bought latex and fashioned a mask, painted and laid hair on it (my own! - I cut a chunk off) and did the show. I ate rotten raw chicken on stage, and terrorised children...bliss! And to top it off we took the play 'on the road' - well - Cockburn! Cockburn is a very small railway village on the South Australian border, forty-seven kilometres from Broken Hill. And it was one of the best theatrical experiences I have ever had!

Megan had been asked to stage the show in the Cockburn Community Hall, and so we all packed up a couple of cars with costumes and whatever props we really needed. We arrived there early and set up. There was no stage and no wings - we would enter from the kitchen on stage right and the veranda to the rear and stage left. It would be commando theatre - we set it to fit the space - nowhere to hide! True excitement!

The audience started to arrive - and kept coming. So many people from other small towns and properties. More chairs were added; our stage shrank. Intimate is too small a word! But it was so good! The audience were so appreciative! They laughed, clapped and gasped - and all no more than five feet away! You cannot buy that experience!

The best anecdote from B&B took place in Cockburn - and I treasure it!

In the final act, the Beast sits slumped over the table, near death. He's a goner! Unless Beauty comes back and saves him. Well, there I was, face down in my chair at the table waiting for Beauty to rush in from stage left door (outside to the verandah) and romantically, dramatically save me. I collapsed - the audience watched silently waiting - waiting - waiting. Finally there was a tap at the window behind the dying beast - and another. I looked up to see - in plain view of the audience - the perfectly coiffed blonde head of Beauty, with an expression of utter embarrassment, looking at me and mouthing through the thick glass, 'The door is locked', pointing to the exterior door. So the dead Beast lumbered up and dramatically stumbled across to the door, unlocked it then stumbled back to his table, collapsed and tried to not crack up as Beauty without missing a beat rushed in to save him - <u>gold</u>! I am still laughing twenty two years later!

Two days later, I was living in Geelong. Seven months later I had moved back, ended up in another music hall this time playing Frank N Furter and actually singing two songs. Then I moved to Adelaide, but came back with Mel in April for ten days to be in *'Cinderella'* as a favor - fun show but no big memories.

I returned briefly from Adelaide in 1996 and my only show was a farce about the Roman Empire *'Rome Sweet Rome'* by Peter Ustinov. None of the reminiscences about this show can be shared (for a multitude of reasons)! It was not the greatest moment in my stage career! Then from 1997, my theatrical career in Adelaide truly took off. I did eleven shows in that year alone, running the full gamut from intense drama to frothy musicals, operetta to arty confrontation shows and short films to PSA's. I had done shows in Her Majesty's theatre to a shoebox where the audience toilets were only accessible via the stage!

I have since directed, choreographed, designed, and produced! And all of it is a direct result of Theatre 44 and the workshop kids.

'Annie Jnr' 2006

by Charles Strauss and Martin Charnin
Marilyn Harris (Director)

Marilyn Harris

A series of musicals became available for junior theatre which included backing CDs (no orchestra needed). As I was involved with schoolkids, I found this a good way to go. I assembled a cast for 'Annie', but found to my chagrin I had to re-cast about half the older actors as they pulled out for various reasons. However, we went on to produce a creditable show.

'Alice in Wonderland Jnr' 2007

Disney
Marilyn Harris (Director)

The cast grew for this show, and we had a great time. I had to cast three 'Alices' as she had to grow and shrink. I made all the costumes as well as directing.

Cast & Crew - Finale 'Annie Jnr' - 2006 Directed by Marilyn Harris

'Wizard of Oz' 2008

by L Frank Baum
Marilyn Harris (Director)

This was my first show without CD provided, so I had to manufacture backings for every song in the score, as we still had no orchestra. Again I made all the costumes. The witch's den scenes were a challenge. We had to show the witch watching the four characters in the woods, so we pre-recorded the action on video and re-played it on a large TV screen (loaned by BigW). The video player failed a couple of times (embarrassing), but in general it worked well.

Then the witch had to fall into the cauldron and shrink. So we had a large barrel with the back cut out and cushions inside. Kayla Honson, as the witch, was pushed in, she crawled out the back, and a smaller 'witch' appeared to try to escape, only to be pushed in and hold up a doll dressed as a witch.

'Cinderella Jnr' 2009

by Rodgers & Hammerstein
Marilyn Harris (Director)

I had an enjoyable time producing and directing the Rodgers and Hammerstein version of '*Cinderella*' in 2009.

In one performance, Cinderella, after going to the ball, (in a superb coach made by Phil Eberle) had to have a costume change before re-entering to serve breakfast to the stepmother and stepsisters. Millie Walker, Shannon Swart and Tilly Balding went on stage to gather around the table for breakfast. However, Bianca Honson (Cinderella) could not remove her hoop petticoat because the knot was too tight. I was called to the dressing room and spent about five minutes or more untying the knot (we could not cut the cord because she had to wear the petticoat again). Meanwhile the three onstage were ad-libbing furiously, talking about the ball, wondering where 'that Cinderella' was, all the time having no idea when she was going to turn up. They did a superb job.

'Seussical Jnr' 2010

by Dr Seuss
Marilyn Harris (Director)

I really loved the challenges of this Dr Seuss piece with so many and varied characters, animals, birds, 'Whos' etc. The funniest part was in the opening performance - the elephant and the bird were holding their joint egg (which was about to hatch into an 'elephant bird') when they dropped it and it rolled off stage.

Tilly Balding—Cat in the Hat—'Seussical' 2010

Maddison Tozer—Horton the Elephant —
'Seussical' 2010

'Shrek the Musical Jnr 2018'

by Jeanine Tesori and David Lindsay-Abaire
Marilyn Harris (Director)

I was delighted to be approached by Willyama High School to direct a play casting some of their students and with the help of several of the teachers. We chose *'Shrek the Musical Jnr'* but could not cast a male Shrek as high school students are reticent to display their talents on stage. So we had a female Shrek, a female donkey and a female Lord Farquaad, who all did a superb job, as did the rest of the cast. We cast, as well as the school students, members of my Glee singing group and members of our Moxie drama group. It was really wonderful to see the cast grow in confidence and I look forward to many more young people gaining similar confidence through their stage appearances.

Theatre Refurbishment 2016

Marilyn Harris

In 2015, we were approached by Sureway, who were providers of the government's 'Work for the Dole' plan. They offered to refurbish Theatre 44 using unemployed people who needed to gain skills. As can be imagined, we accepted the offer gratefully. The theatre was beginning to look rather shabby inside, although the outside had been repainted using a similar scheme in the early 2000s.

Peter Reinhardt was appointed overseer of the project, and he did an excellent job of making the theatre look loved again. I was pleased to work with him and exchange ideas for upgrading.

The theatre interior was painted a dark purple, with the foyer a russet colour. Carpet was laid on the front section of the floor, and the rear section had the old lino removed and the floor painted. The dressing rooms were painted and provided with new benches, mirrors and lights and carpet on the floors and even on the stairways to the stage. The black 'flats' were stripped, and the black material replaced. A wheelchair ramp was installed and the foyer toilets painted.

Broken Hill City Council granted us $9,000 to replace the backstage switchboard, and we now feel much safer without the network of power boards.

A later grant from Broken Hill City Council meant we were able to mount two large gas heaters on the rear wall, which are very effective. With the air conditioners repaired, the theatre was comfortable.

My Work With Rep

Marilyn Harris

Since I have been with the theatre, I have been director of close to fifty shows of various kinds. I have, for the past four years, run Moxie drama club each Sunday morning for kids aged eight to fifteen years. What keeps me going? I think it is the pleasure of seeing kids grow in confidence as they learn to interact with others of like passion and perform on stage. To see a child burst into tears at their first performance, only to come back for more and grow into a starring role, has been a source of great joy to me and those I work with. Parents from time to time have told me how their children have developed in confidence at school after being a member of Moxie.

My husband, John Harris, has worked alongside me for most of these shows in one capacity or another. He now has charge of the sound desk, and from a complete beginner has made himself proficient in that area, in consultation with our son, Glendon, who is an audio engineer.

Sanny Dougherty has also been a great backstop of recent years. Sanny choreographs dances and is the best 'dresser' and organiser of kids backstage.

I hope you can see, as I can, the difference Repertory has made in the lives of so many people. The chance to express themselves, to grow in confidence, to entertain others, to learn to work as a team, and to experience a creative outlet like no other - these are what has kept Repertory going for seventy five years.

Life Members of Broken Hill Repertory Society Inc.

Brian Adkins

Doug Banks

June Marie Bennett

Bob Browne

Robert Cawdle

Rosemary Clarke

Frank Coorey

Marilyn Harris

Ron Herriman

Camille Jenkins

Dick Kelly

David Lee

Don Mudie

Airlie Pedlar

Peter Sweeney

Merv Tucker

Eleanor Williams

Ken Arnall

John Barrett

Paul Brady

Denise Carroll

Bob Clarke

Ann Clarke

Ann Gordon

Megan Hendy

Faye Herriman

Doug Jones

Ruth Kelly

Kay McLachlan

Geoff Olds

John Pickup

Muriel Theo

Rodger Wallace

Peter Rayner Kevin Whitby Sandra Williams Ted Drane

Roger Ralph David Semon Carol Ware Mark Ellis

Brian Richardson Mary Stewart Quentin Wills Don Denham

Phil Smithers Alan Tonkin Kern Webb John Edingburgh

Peter Sweeney Leigh Tucker Robert Warren Michael Eddy

Bill Stevenson Jeff Vaughan Barbara Yelland Nesta Emmett

Francine Skewes Steve Wignall Greg Eddy

Marie Separovitch Lovina Williams Kim Dunlew Renate Ergis

Pat Smith Phil Williams Peter Ellis Peter Forde

Graeme Strauss Alan Streade Jack Ditchburn Chris Falkner

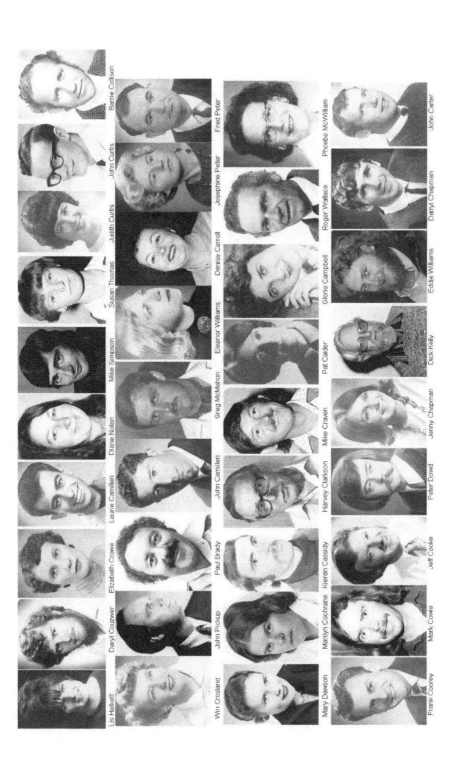

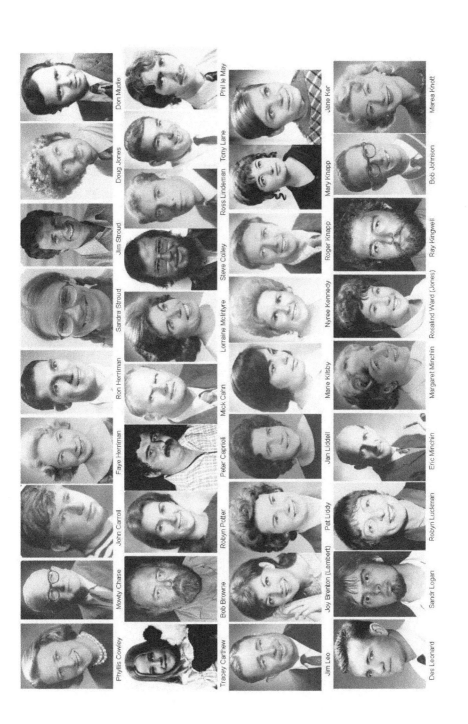

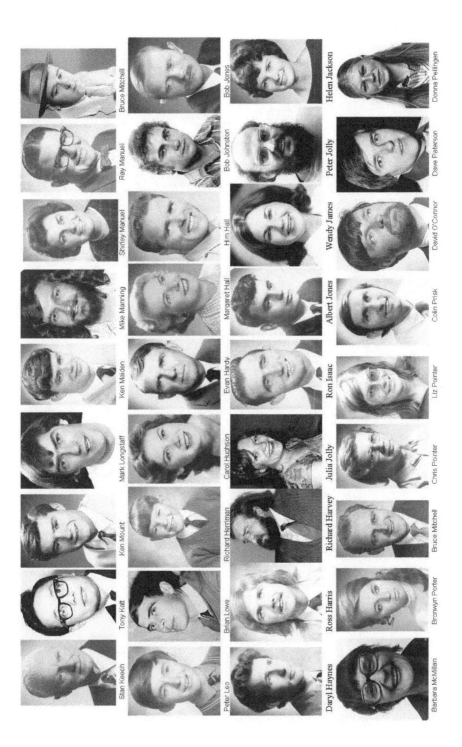

Edith Moore
Gail McLean
Graeme Nilsen
Gwendoline Neeson
Jane Mann
Jill McDonald
Jill Newton-McLeod
Judith Beritt
Judith Parsons

Kath Pugh
Ken McGann
Lachlan Peter
Leah McCubbin
Margaret McKay
Margaret Noonan
Maria O'Regan
Marion Power
Moira Magee

Pam Olney
Pauline McMahon
Peter McLeod
Peter Pascoe
Peter Perry
Raelene Neate
Ralph Madsen
Robyn Plimer
Ross Phillips

Giles Waterman
Vicky Pogulis
Josephine Peoples
Grace Pincell
Rod Brookes
Rhonda Curver
Christian Lalder
Arthur Day
Bob Devine

Broken Hill Repertory Society Inc.

ACTORS & DIRECTORS
1990-2000

Miles Philpott, Judy Philpott, Tony Morgan, Tom McReynolds, Sue McGlinchey, Stewart Menzies, Rick Clay, Diane Dimbrell, Brian Debnam, Keryan Dunn

Alana Robertson, Bob Russell, Malcolm Robinson, Chris Rankin, Lis Rae, Jocelyn Robinson, Jacqui Rich, Helen Post, David Paterson, Ray Pickering

Genny Philip, Charmaine Adams, Craig Brealey, Peter Forde, Alicia Elliott

Megan Hendy (Pollard), Matthew Huxtable, Matthew West, Ruth Quick (Kelly), Marilyn Harris, Adrian 'Aj' Bartley, John Barrett

Bob Clarke, Rosemary Clarke, Corey Page

Broken Hill Repertory Society Inc.
ACTORS & DIRECTORS 2001-2016

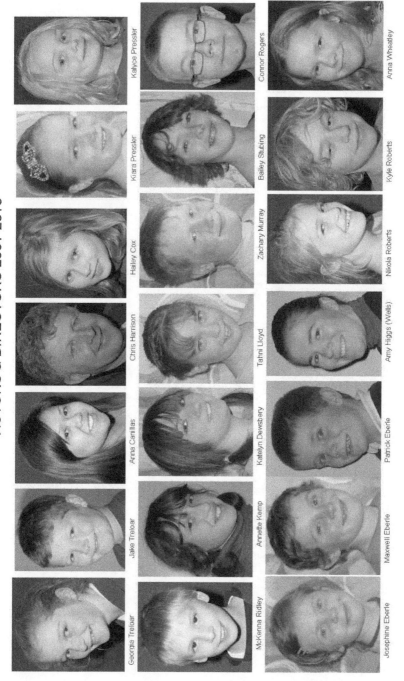

Georgia Treloar

Jake Treloar

Anna Canillas

Chris Harrison

Hailey Cox

Kiara Pressler

Kalyce Pressler

McKenna Ridley

Annette Kemp

Katelyn Dewsbery

Tahni Lloyd

Zachary Murray

Bailey Stubing

Connor Rogers

Josephine Eberle

Maxwell Eberle

Patrick Eberle

Amy Higgs (Wells)

Nikola Roberts

Kyle Roberts

Anna Wheatley

Actors & Directors 1990-2000

Matthew McAvaney · Airlie Pedlar · Zara Ferguson · Jazmine De Main · Corinne Barratt · Marj Collison · Bob Johnson · Brooke Kowalski · Richard Tosen

Carol McGavisk · Cameron Marshall · Barry Cosman · Alison Wythe (Former) · Mitchell Harris · Glendon Harris · Andrew Harris · Serenna Shutt · Peter Dowd

Diane Cotterill · Poppy Garner · Tonya Garner · Ann Clarke · June Bennett · Robert Marcon · Bert Henry · Phoebe McWilliam · Pauline Hendy · Keith Chilman

Stacey Hendy (Webb) · Bronwyn Canon · Cameron Koch · Andrew Spencer · Nathan McBain · Andrew Barrett · Ian Backhouse · Jason Kowalski

Broken Hill Repertory Society Inc.
ACTORS & DIRECTORS
2001-2016

Catherine Bransdon
Shannon Swart
Nathan Hughes
Shona Swart
Jessica Hughes
Emma Chaplyn
George Chaplyn
Declan Swart
Stephanie Turley
Jayden Lee
Titus Maddern
Stephanie Finnis
Caitlin Lee
Hamish Spiteri
Samantha Limbert
Emma Clarke
Sophie Morrison
Kiana Anderson
Jake Spain
Nellie Hicks
Anita Okello
Ellysia Oldsen

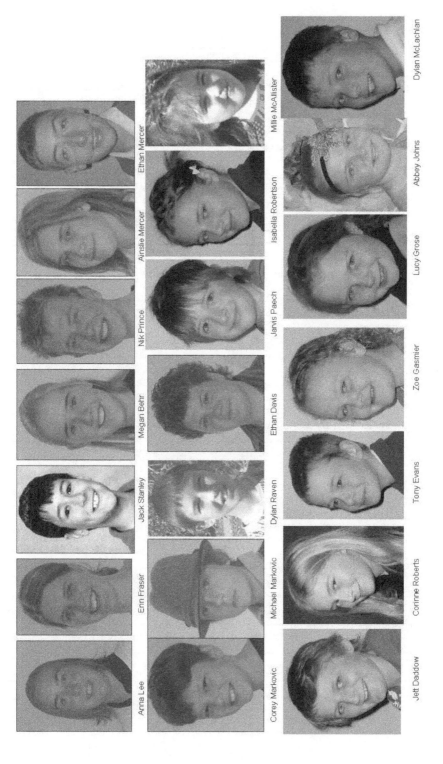

Year		Production	Author/Composer	Director
1944	1	The Wind and the Rain	Merton Hodge	Victor Bindley
1945	2	The Women	Clare Boothe Luce	Victor Bindley
	3	Ambrose Applejohn's Adventure	Walter Hacket	Victor Bindley
	4	The Ghost Train	Arnold Ridley	Victor Bindley
	5	Private Lives	Noel Coward	Victor Bindley
	6	Arms and the Man	George Bernard Shaw	Victor Bindley
	7	The Middle Watch	Ian Hay	Victor Bindley
1946	8	Yes, My Darling Daughter	Mark Reed	Victor Bindley
	9	Outward Bound	Sutton Vane	Victor Bindley
	10	Fledglings	Adapted by Vic Bindley	Victor Bindley
	11	A Bill of Divorcement	Clemence Dane	Victor Bindley
1947	12	The Hasty Heart	Captain John Patrick	Victor Bindley
	13	Banana Ridge	Ben Travers	Victor Bindley
	14	Murder at the Ministry	F L Cary & A A Thomson	Victor Bindley
	15	Winterset	Maxwell Anderson	Victor Bindley
	16	The Cuckoo in the Nest	Ben Travers	Victor Bindley
	17	The Bat	Rinehart & Hopwood	Victor Bindley
1948	18	Amphritryon 38	Jean Giraudoux	Victor Bindley
	19	Rope	Patrick Hamilton	Murray Gordon
	20	Three Men on a Horse	Holm & Abbott	Bert Johns
	21	Kind Lady	Edward Chodorov	Marion Henry
	22	Hay Fever	Noel Coward	Mark Howard
	23	Dangerous Corner	J B Priestley	Bill Spencer
1949	24	Quiet Weekend	Esther McCracken	Bob Gluyas
	25	Anonymous Lover	Vernon Sylvaine	Bill Spencer
	26	Suspect	Percy & Denton	Bill Spencer
	27	The Golden Fleece	J B Priestley	Marion Henry
	28	Ten Little Niggers	Agatha Christie	Rex Saggers
	29	To Have the Honour	A A Milne	Brian Grosvenor
1950	30	Misanthrope/Doctor in Spite	Moliere	Roy Williams
	31	Arsenic and Old Lace	Joseph Kesselring	Brian Grosvenor
	32	Ladies in Retirement	Denham & Percy	Dennis Swan
	33	Mungo's Mansion	Walter Macken	Tom Davoren
	34	The Chiltern Hundreds	William Douglas Home	Marion Henry
	35	Candied Peel	Falkland L Cary	Bill Spencer
1951	36	Flare Path	Terence Rattigan	Rex Saggers
	37	Mr Pimm Passes By	A A Milne	Cliff Neate
	38	The Guinea Pigs	Warren Chatham Strode	Marion Henry
	39	Blithe Spirit	Noel Coward	Brian Grosvenor
	40	Fools Rush In	Kenneth Home	Cliff Neate
	41	On Monday Next	Philip King	J Hampel & J McBeath
1952	42	Bonaventure	Charlotte Hastings	Marion Henry
	43	The Little Foxes	Lilian Helleman	Dennis Swan
	44	Night Must Fall	Emlyn Williams	Brian Grosvenor
	45	Present Laughter	Noel Coward	Cliff Neate
	46	George and Margaret	Gerald Savory	Drusie Cox
	47	Someone at the Door	D & C Christie	Cliff Neate & Hugh Knox
1953	48	They Came to a City	J B Priestley	Jack Ditchburn
	49	Little Lambs Eat Ivy	Noel Langley	Wally Larn

	50	The Patsy	Barry Conners	Bill Spencer
	51	The Merchant of Venice	Shakespeare	Jack Firth
	52	Black Limelight	Gordon Sherry	John Hampel
	53	Castles in the Air	Alan Melville	Cliff Neate & Wally Larn
1954	54	The Two Mrs Carrolls	Martin Vale	Drusie Cox
	55	Lovers' Leap	Philip Johnson	Brian Grosvenor
	56	Grand National Night	D & C Christie	Cliff Neate
	57	The Happiest Days of Your Life	John Dighton	John Hampel
	58	Message for Margaret	James Parish	Drusie Cox
1955	59	Private Lives	Noel Coward	Marion Henry
	60	Hobson's Choice	Harold Brighouse	John Settle & Marg Hall
	61	The Man From the Ministry	Madeleine Bingham	John Hampel
	62	Young Wives Tale	Ronald Jeans	Margaret Hall
	63	The Late Edwina Black	Dinner & Morum	Max Middleton
	64	Lady be Careful	Stafford Dickens	Hartley Williams
1956	65	Dial M for Murder	Frederick Knott	Drusie Cox
	66	While the Sun Shines	Terence Rattigan	Margaret Hall
	67	Easy Money	Arnold Ridley	George Rainsford
	68	An Inspector Calls	J B Priestley	B Hyland & M Middleton
	69	Outward Bound	Sutton Vane	George Rainsford
	70	The Ex Mrs Y	Eyton & Melford	Don Vincent
1957	71	If This Be Error	Rachel Grieve	Hartley Williams
	72	We Proudly Present	Ivor Novello	G Rainsford & B Mitchell
	73	The Admirable Crichton	J M Barrie	Brian Grosvenor
	74	Someone Waiting	Emlyn Williams	Bruce Mitchell
	75	White Sheep of the Family	Du Garde Peach & Ian Hay	J Ditchburn & F Herriman
	76	Love from a Stranger	Frank Vosper (Agatha Christi	Helen Hoban & Stan Turner
1958	77	One Wild Oat	Vernon Sylvaine	M Hall & H Williams
	78	A Murder Has Been Arranged	Emlyn Williams	Don Vincent
	79	Doctor in the House	Ted Willis (Richard Gordon)	Brian Grosvenor
	80	Rebecca	Daphne du Maurier	Fae Herriman
	81	Sit Down a Minute, Adrian	Jevan Brandon-Thomas	D Vincent & M Middleton
	82	The Gioconda Smile	Aldous Huxley	Helen Hoban
1959	83	Will Any Gentleman	Vernon Sylvaine	George Rainsford
	84	The Gift	Mary Lumsden	Max Middleton
	85	The Wooden Dish	Edmund Morris	Max Greaves
	86	Reluctant Heroes	Colin Morris	John Ditchburn
	87	Granite	Clemence Dane	H Hoban & E Williams
	88	Dear Charles	Alan Melville	Fae Herriman
1960	89	Witness for the Prosecution	Agatha Christie	Eleanor Williams
	90	The Importance of Being Ernest	Oscar Wilde	Don Neville
	91	The Shifting Heart	Richard Beynon	Eleanor Williams
	92	Sailor, Beware!	King & Carey	M Hall & J Ditchborn
	93	The Man From the Ministry	Mal Dinelli	B Cawdle & G Gammon
	94	Ours Is a Nice House	John Clevedon	Judy Graham
1961	95	Traveller Without Luggage	Jean Anouih	Helen Hoban
	96	The Bride and the Bachelor	Ronald Millar	H Hoban & J Ditchburn
	97	Madam Tic Tac	Cary & Weathers	Bob Cawdle
	98	Only an Orphan Girl	Henning Nelms	Ginsey Gammon
	99	Our Town	Thornton Wilder	Fae Herriman

	100	The Tender Trap	Shulman & Smith	Margaret Hall
1962	101	Me and My Girl	Rose, Ferber, Gay	Don Neville
	102	All for Mary (billed 100th prod)	Brooke & Bannerman	Margaret Hall
	103	The Diary of Anne Frank	Goorich & Hackett	Eleanor Williams
	104	Book of the Month	Basil Thomas	Kay McLachlan
	105	Open House (Opening Theatre 44)	Philip Mackie	Bob Cawdle
	106	Deep are the Roots	D'Usseau & Gow	H Hoban & E Minchin
1963	107	Oklahoma	Rodgers & Hammerstein	Williams, Neville, Martin
	108	Libel	Edward Wooll	B Cawdle & J Pickup
	109	Towards Zero	Agatha Christie	P Calder & E Minchin
	110	The Rape of the Belt	Benn W Levy	Kay McLachlan
	111	A Streetcar Named Desire	Tenessee Williams	Fae Herriman
	112	The Reluctant Debutante	William Douglas Home	Pat Calder
1964	113	The Roaring Days	John Pickup/Roy Mitchell	Pickup, Williams, Martin
	114	The Harp in the South	Ruth Park & Leslie Rees	Kay McLachlan
	115	The Sleeping Prince	Terence Rattigan	Eugenie Bond
	116	Teahouse of the August Moon	Patrick/Sneider	Pat Calder
	117	The Blue Goose	Peter Blackmore	Brian Martin
	118	All My Sons	Arthur Miller	Frank McKone
1965	119	South Pacific	Rodgers & Hammerstein	Cawdle, Bond, Williams
	120	Anastasia	Mouriette, adapt. Bolton	Eugenie Bond
	121	Six Months' Grace	Morley/Hamilton	Ken Arnall
	122	Moby Dick Rehearsed	Orson Welles	John Pickup
	123	The Amorous Prawn	Anthony Kimmins	Tom McReynolds
	-	Friday Night Revue	Brian Martin, Bill Bentley	Brian Martin
	124	Picnic	William Inge	Peter Sweeney
1966	125	The Sentimental Bloke	C J Dennis/Albert Arlen	McLachlan, Martin, Williams
	126	Sunday Cost 5 Pesos/Happy Journey/Hiss the Villian		Rich,Green,Curtis
	127	The Crucible	Arthur Miller	Ken Arnall
	128	Wanted - One Body	Raymond Dyer	Peter Sweeney
	129	A Spring Song	Ray Matthew	Kay McLachlan
	130	The Mad Woman of Chaillot	Jean Giraudoux	Trevor, Green, Miller
1967	131	Showboat	Kern & Hammerstein	Martin, Barrett, Williams
	132	See How They Run	Philip King	Peter Sweeney
	133	Summer of the Seventeenth Doll	Ray Lawler	Barbara Arnall
	134	My Three Angels	Sam & Bella Spewack	Bob Clarke
	135	Of Mice and Men	John Steinbeck	Fae Herriman
	136	You Can't Take it With You	Kaufman and Hart	Kay McLachlan
1968	137	Tom Jones	Henry Fielding	John Pickup
	138	Boeing Boeing	Marc Camoletti	John Curtis
	139	The One Day of the Year	Alan Seymour	Beryl Green
	140	Romanoff and Juliet	Peter Ustinov	David O'Connor
	141	An Enemy of the People	Ibsen, adapt. Miller	Miles Philpott
	142	Say Who You Are	Waterhouse & Hall	John Barrett
1969	143	Peter Pan	J M Barrie	K Finlayson, E Minchin
	144	Simon and Laura	Alan Melville	John Curtis
	145	A Day in the Death of Joe Egg	Peter Nicholls	Pat Calder
	146	Don't Utter a Note	Anton Delmar	J Guthrie, P Perry
	147	A Man For All Seasons	Robert Bolt	Barbara Arnall
	148	Under the Yum Yum Tree	Lawrence Roman	Riet Kilsby

1970	149	Cinderella	Crocker & Gilder	Kate Finlayson
	150	French Polish		
		First One Act Play Festival - The Bespoke Overcoat		
	151	Murder in the Cathedral	T S Eliot	
	152	The Odd Couple	Neil Simon	
	153	A Taste of Honey	Shelagh Delaney	
	154	The Killing of Sister George	Frank Marcus	
1971	155	Irma La Douce	Monnot & Breffort	
	156	Chase Me, Comrade	Ray Cooney	
	157	Night of January 16th	Ayn Rand	
		One Act Play Festival - A Dead Liberty		
	158	Who's Afraid of Virginia Woolf?	Edward Albee	
	159	I'll Get my Man	Philip King	
1972	160	Aladdin		
	161	No Time for Fig Leaves	Greenwood & King	
	162	Come Blow Your Horn	Neil Simon	
	163	A Hatful of Rain	Michael V Gazzo	
	164	She's Done it Again	Lloyd Lonergan	
	165	Dimboola	Jack Hibberd	
1973	166	Dick Whittington		
	167	Auntie Mame	Jerry Hermon	
		One Act Play Festival - In Camera		
	168	Once In a Blue Moon	John Dole	
	169	The Physicists	Friedrick Durrenmatt	
	170	The Lion in Winter	James Goldman	
	171	The Hollow	Agatha Christie	
1974	172	Snow White & the Seven Dwarfs		
	173	Arsenic and Old Lace	Joseph Kesselring	
	174	The Children's Hour	Lillian Hellman	
	175	Barefoot in the Park	Neil Simon	
	176	The Taming of the Shrew	Shakespeare	
	177	Alice in Wonderland		
	178	The Anniversary		
1975	179	The Pyjama Game	Adler/Ross/Abbott/Bissell	
	180	Twelve Angry Men	Reginald Rose	
	181	The Sound of Music	Rodgers & Hammerstein	Don Whiting
		One Act Play Festival - These Walls of Ours		
	182	Who Goes Bare?	Darbon & Harris	
	183	The Ghost Train	Arnold Ridley	
1976	184	Strange Journey		
	185	Don's Party	David Williamson	
	186	Beauty and the Beast		
	187	The Last of the Knucklemen	John Powers	
1977	188	Jack and the Beanstalk		
	189	Reedy River	Dick Diamond	
		One Act Play Festival - The Happy Journey/Zoo Story		
	190	Prisoner of Second Avenue	Neil Simon	
1978	191	Dirty Work at the Crossroads	Bill Johnson	
	192	Coralie Lansdowne Says No	Alex Buzo	
	193	Ten Little Niggers	Agatha Christie	

	194	Oliver	Lionel Bart	Marge Collison
	195	Wizard of Oz	Baum, Arlen, Harburg	
1979	196	Oh! What a Lovely War	Joan Littlewood	
	197	This Old Man Comes Rolling Home	Dorothy Hewett	
	198	A Bird in the Hand	Derek Benfield	
	199	The King & I (billed as 200th prod)	Rodgers & Hammerstein	Marge Collison
	200	Flying Sorcery	Al Stewart	
1980	201	Annie Get Your Gun	Berlin/Fields	Finlayson/Barrett
	202	Jugglers 3		
		One Act Play Festival - Dust is the Heart		
	203	One Flew Over the Cuckoo's Nest	Dale Wasserman	
	204	Bedroom Farce	Alan Ayckbourn	
	205	Tell Tale Murder	P Weathers	
1981	206	Legend of King O'Malley	Bob Ellis & Michael Boddy	
	207	Gaslight	Patrick Hamilton	
	208	The Club	David Williamson	
	209	Have You Any Dirty Washing	Clive Exton	
1982	210	Cinderella		Camille Jenkins
	211	Not Now, Darling	Ray Cooney & John Chapman	
1983	212	Trap for a Lonely Man		
		One Act Play Festival - Fluff		
	213	Snow White		Camille Jenkins
	214	Old Time Music Hall		
	215	Deathtrap	Ira Levin	
	216	Travelling North	David Williamson	
	217	Double Laugh/Between Mouthful/Black Comedy		
1984	218	On Our Selection	Edmund Duggan	
1985		Not available		
1986		Not available		
1987		Not available		
1988		Hello Dolly (Rep-Harmonic)	Jerry Hermon	Bob Browne
		Charlie and the Chocolate Factory	Roald Dahl	Rosemary Clarke
1989		That's Entertainment		Muriel Theo
		Carousel (Rep-Harmonic)	Rodgers & Hammerstein	Muriel Theo/June Langford
1990		My Three Angels	Samuel & Bella Spewack	Bob Clarke
		Aladdin		Rosemary Clarke
		One Act Play Festival		
		This is It		Marilyn Harris
1991		Babes in the Wood	John Bartlett	Muriel Theo
		That's Entertainment		Muriel Theo
1992		No Business Like Show Business		Marilyn Harris/Megan Hendy
		Mikado (Rep-Harmonic)	Gilbert & Sullivan	Marilyn Harris
		Space Demons		Megan Hendy
1993		Join the Circus		Marilyn Harris
		Festival 4 - Lady Killers	William Rose	Megan Hendy
		- Teddy Bears Picnic	Ernie Nolan	Matthew Huxtable
		- Streets		John Barrett
1993		The Removalists	David Williamson	Paul Brady
		Showboat	Kern/Hammerstein	Muriel Theo

1994	Beauty and the Beast	Ashman/Rice	Megan Hendy
1995	The Sunshine Boys	Neil Simon	Rosemary Clarke
	The Age of Aquarius		Megan Hendy
	Oklahoma	Rodgers & Hammerstein	Marilyn Harris
1996	Rome Sweet Rome	James Erwin	Charmaine Adams
	Blabbermouth	Mary Morris/Gleitzman	Michele Kowalski
	...in Concert		Marilyn Harris
	Sleeping Beauty		Charmaine Adams
1997	Jack and the Beanstalk		Rosemary Clarke
1998	Not available		
1999	Not available		
2000	Not available		
2001	When the Wind Blows		Rosemary Clarke
	Music From the Movies		Marilyn Harris
2002	Save Theatre 44 Variety Show		Muriel Theo & June Bennett
	Variety Showcase		Xanthe Edgecumbe
2004	Winter Spectacular		Marilyn Harris
	Rocky Horror Picture Show	Jim Sharman	Andrew Bevarne
	The Wild West		
	Twelve Angry Men	Reginald Rose	Matt Palmer
2005	Fairytale Spectacular		Marilyn Harris
	Battle of the Bands		
	Broadway Spectacular		Mariyn
	Bugsy Malone	Alan Park/Paul Williams	Willyama High School
2006	Aussie Radio Show		Marilyn Harris
	Hitlers Daughter		Monkey Baa
	Class Act (HSc Music Students)		Marilyn Harris
	Annie Jnr	Strouse & Charnin	Marilyn Harris
	Sentimental Journey		Marilyn Harris
2007	Alice in Wonderland Jnr	Disney	Marilyn Harris
	Happy Days		Marilyn Harris
2008	Wizard of Oz	Baum, Arlen, Harburg	Marilyn Harris
	Stage 'n' Screen		Marilyn Harris
2009	Cinderella Jnr	Rodgers & Hammerstein	Marilyn Harris
	Once Upon a Time		Marilyn Harris
	Believe (dance)		Joy Baldwin
	Monkey Baa workshop		
	Christmas Cheer		Katrina Walker
2010	BH Pop Stars		Marilyn Harris
	Swingin' Sixties		Marilyn Harris
	Seussical the Musical	Ahrens & Flaherty	Marilyn Harris
	Looking Back		Marilyn Harris
	Fiddler on the Roof	Bock & Harnick	Katrina Walker
2011	Animation Sensation		Marilyn Harris
	Theatre Games		David Lee
	Covenant Players Workshop		
	Drama Group Play		Ethan Mercer
	Broadway concert		Marilyn Harris
	Christmas Concert		Paulette Mercer
2012	One Act Plays		Corey Page

		Legends		Marilyn Harris
		Short & Sweet Workshop		
		Woden Valley Youth Choir		
		Skits		Tom Morrison
		Sound of Movies		Marilyn Harris
		Short & Sweet Workshop (plays)		
		Christmas Concert		Paulette Mercer
2013		Broadway concert		Marilyn Harris
		A Bit o' Drama (Moxie)		Marilyn Harris
		Blues in the Night		Marilyn Harris
		Hot Aussie Christmas		Marilyn Harris
2014		Forties Favourites		Marilyn Harris
		Fairytale Spectacular		Marilyn Harris
		Rinse the Blood off my Toga (Moxie)		Marilyn Harris
		Pop U Love		Marilyn Harris
2015		The Way We Were		Marilyn Harris
		Dramafest incl 'Ice Cream Cart'		Marilyn Harris
		Fairytale Spectacular		Marilyn Harris
		Hot Aussie Christmas		Marilyn Harris
2016		Theatre Warming (refurbishment - Sureway)		Marilyn Harris
		Long Hair & Flares		Marilyn Harris
		Fairytale Spectacular		Marilyn Harris
2017		Broadway Spectacular		Marilyn Harris
		Remember This		Marilyn Harris
		Fairytale Spectacular		Marilyn Harris
		The Letter	W Somerset Maugham	Luke Cripps
		Hot Aussie Christmas		Marilyn Harris
2018		Cinema Celebration		Marilyn Harris
		Shrek Jnr	Tesori & Lindsay-Abaire	Marilyn Harris (Willyama)
		Drought Relief Concert		Marilyn Harris
		Hot Aussie Christmas		Marilyn Harris

CPSIA information can be obtained
at www.ICGtesting.com
Printed in the USA
BVHW071154240619
551796BV00004B/537/P